OUR WORLD IN PICTURES
THE DINOSAURS BOOK

WRITTEN BY **JOHN WOODWARD**
CONSULTANT **DARREN NAISH**

SECOND EDITION
DK Delhi
Senior Editor Dharini Ganesh
Project Art Editor Anjali Sachar
DTP Coordinator Vishal bhatia
Jacket Designer Tanya Mehrotra
Senior Jackets Coordinator Priyanka Sharma Saddi
Senior DTP Designer Harish Aggarwal
DTP Designer Anita Yadav
Pre-production Manager Balwant Singh
Production Manager Pankaj Sharma
Senior Managing Editor Rohan Sinha
Managing Art Editor Sudakshina Basu
Editorial Head Glenda Fernandes
Design Head Malavika Talukder

DK London
Managing Editor Rachel Fox
Managing Art Editor Owen Peyton Jones
Production Editor Robert Dunn
Production Controller Laura Andrews
Jacket Design Development Manager Sophia MTT
Publisher Andrew Macintyre
Associate Publishing Director Liz Wheeler
Art Director Karen Self
Publishing Director Jonathan Metcalf
Consultant Prof Paul Barrett

FIRST EDITION
DK Delhi
Senior Editor Anita Kakar
Senior Art Editor Stuti Tiwari Bhatia
Assistant Art Editor Ankita Sharma
Jacket Designers Suhita Dharamjit, Juhi Sheth
Jackets Editorial Coordinator Priyanka Sharma
Pre-production Manager Balwant Singh
Production Manager Pankaj Sharma
Senior Managing Editor Rohan Sinha
Managing Art Editor Sudakshina Basu

DK London
Senior Editors Shaila Brown, Ben Morgan
Senior Art Editor Jacqui Swan
Jacket Editor Amelia Collins
Jacket Designer Surabhi Wadhwa-Gandhi
Jacket Design Development Manager Sophia MTT
Picture Researcher Jo Walton
Managing Editor Lisa Gillespie
Managing Art Editor Owen Peyton Jones
Publisher Andrew Macintyre
Art Director Karen Self
Associate Publishing Director Liz Wheeler
Design Director Phil Omerod
Publishing Director Jonathan Metcalf

This edition published in 2023
First published in Great Britain in 2018
by Dorling Kindersley Limited
DK, One Embassy Gardens, 8 Viaduct Gardens, London SW11 7BW

The authorised representative in the EEA is
Dorling Kindersley Verlag GmbH. Arnulfstr. 124, 80636 Munich, Germany

Copyright © 2018, 2023 Dorling Kindersley Limited
A Penguin Random House Company
10 9 8 7 6 5 4 3 2 1
001–334050–June/2023

A CIP catalogue record for this book is available from the British Library.
ISBN: 978-0-2416-0165-5

Printed and bound in China

For the curious
www.dk.com

MIX
Paper | Supporting
responsible forestry
FSC™ C018179

This book was made with Forest Stewardship
Council™ certified paper – one small step
in DK's commitment to a sustainable future.
For more information go to
www.dk.com/our-green-pledge

CONTENTS

BEFORE THE DINOSAURS 28

OUR WORLD IN PICTURES

THE DINOSAURS BOOK

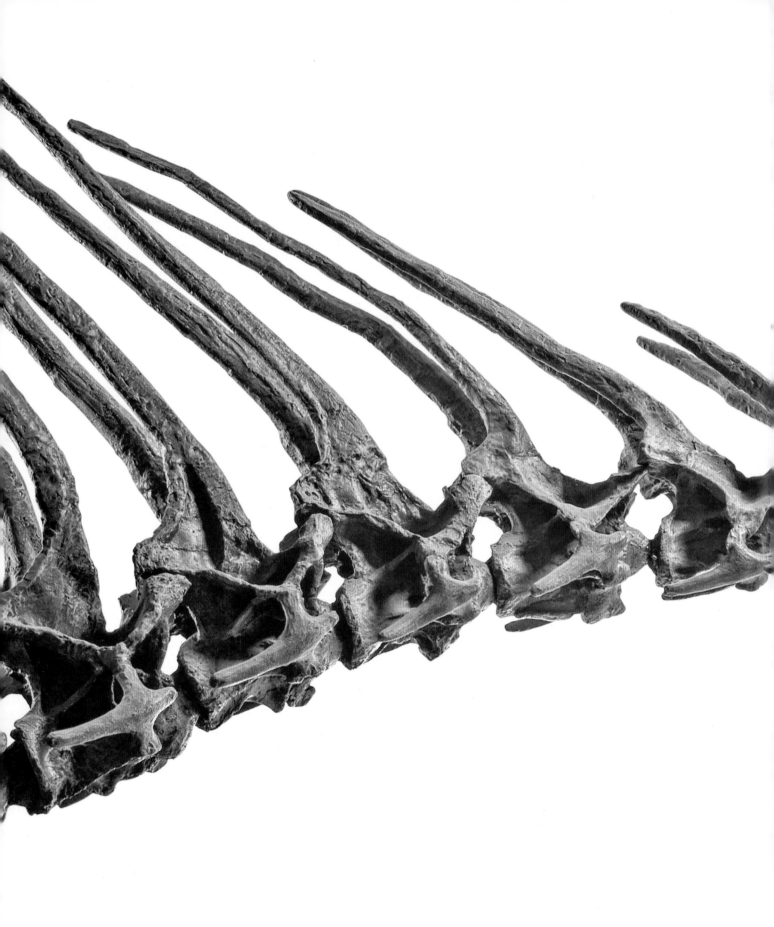

Styracosaurus

Pachycephalosaurus

Gigantspinosaurus

Foreword

The amazing variety of life that exists on our planet is so rich that new kinds of organism are still being discovered every day. More than 2 million species (types of organism) have been named and described by scientists, and there are probably millions more waiting to be discovered. But these are only a tiny fraction of the species that have ever existed on Earth in the past. If you were to go back in time 100 million years, you would find yourself surrounded by just as many different animals and plants as today, but – unless you had read this book first – you wouldn't recognize any of them.

Until a little over two centuries ago, no one realized this. They thought that the animals they saw around them had always existed, and that the world hadn't really changed over time. But in the late 18th century, scientists started examining strange shapes found in rocks and realized that they were fossils – the remains of ancient life that had been turned to stone. Most of these fossils were of seashells and other familiar forms, but some were dramatically different – huge bones, skulls, and teeth of gigantic animals that lived millions of years before the dawn of human history.

Using fossils that date right back to the beginning of life on Earth, about 3,800 million years ago, scientists have been able to piece together most of the history of life. One of the most exciting part of that story started about 230 million years ago with the earliest dinosaurs. Over the following 164 million years, these animals were to evolve into the most spectacular land animals that have

Sciadophyton

Phlegethontia

Corythosaurus

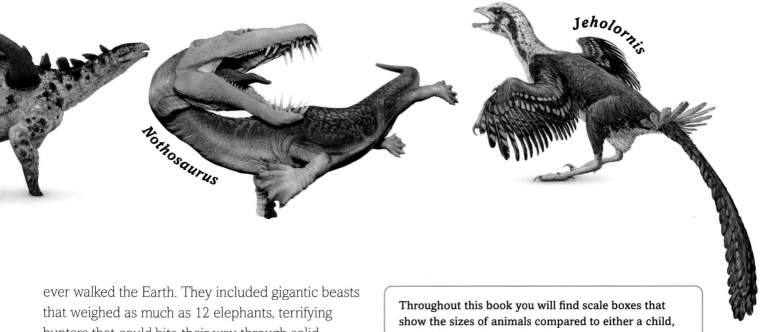
Nothosaurus

Jeholornis

ever walked the Earth. They included gigantic beasts that weighed as much as 12 elephants, terrifying hunters that could bite their way through solid bone, and strange creatures with horns, frills, and even feathers.

The giant dinosaurs were wiped out in a global catastrophe 66 million years ago. But their fossils survive, along with other fossils that show, beyond doubt, that many of their smaller, feathery relatives were able to fly. Some of these feathered dinosaurs survived the disaster to flourish in the new era as birds. So, not only do fossils tell us about life in the distant past – they can also reveal astonishing facts about animals that we see all around us every day.

John Woodward

Throughout this book you will find scale boxes that show the sizes of animals compared to either a child, a school bus, or human hand.

Child = 1.45 m
(4 ft 9 in) tall

School bus = 11 m
(36 ft) wide

Hand = 16 cm
(6 in) long

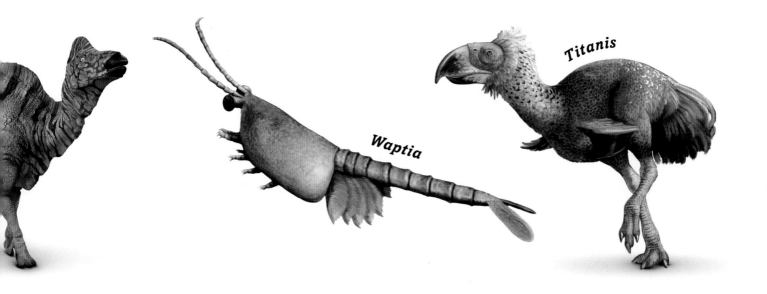
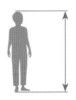

Waptia

Titanis

Timeline of life

The story of life on Earth is written in the rocks. Over millions of years, sediments like sand and clay settle on the floors of lakes and seas and harden to form layer after layer of sedimentary rock. Trapped in these ancient deposits are the fossilized remains of prehistoric organisms, with each layer capturing a snapshot of life from a different period in history.

KEY

Early Earth

Paleozoic Era

Mesozoic Era

Cenozoic Era

Million years ago **MYA**

▶ 252–201 MYA

Triassic
Reptiles ruled the world in the Triassic. They gave rise to the first dinosaurs, the first flying reptiles, and the first true mammals, which were little bigger than shrews. Crocodiles and turtles appeared, and the giant aquatic reptiles cruised the seas.

Austriadactylus

▶ 201–145 MYA

Jurassic
The Jurassic saw the rise of the colossal plant-eating sauropod dinosaurs such as *Brachiosaurus*, as well as the giant meat-eating theropods that preyed on them. Smaller theropods evolved into the first birds. Deserts shrank, and forests of conifer trees, monkey puzzles, and ferns spread across the land.

Allosaurus

299–252 MYA ◀

Permian
Earth's climate dried out in the Permian and deserts replaced forest. Reptiles and related animals called synapsids were the dominant land animals. Unlike amphibians, which breed in water, reptiles laid waterproof eggs and could breed on land. At the end of the Permian, most of Earth's species were wiped out, possibly due to a rise in global temperatures and major changes in seawater chemistry.

Moschops

Edaphosaurus

4.6–0.5 billion years ago

Precambrian
The Precambrian is a supereon that makes up nearly nine-tenths of Earth's history. For most of it, the only life forms were single-celled organisms in the sea, such as cyanobacteria. Fossilized imprints of much larger, leaf-shaped organisms that might have been animals appear about 600 million years ago. Known as the Ediacaran organisms, these mysterious life forms vanished at the end of the Precambrian.

Cyanobacteria

▶ 541–484 MYA

Cambrian
A wide range of new animal fossils appear in rocks from the Cambrian Period. A sudden burst of evolution – the Cambrian explosion – seems to have produced animals with the first limbs, heads, sense organs, shells, and exoskeletons. All the major categories of invertebrate alive today originated in the Cambrian, from molluscs and arthropods to echinoderms such as *Helicoplacus* (a relative of starfish).

Helicoplacus

Geological periods

Earth's history stretches back 4.6 billion years. This vast span of time is divided into long sections called eras, which are divided in turn into shorter sections called periods. The Jurassic Period, for instance, is when many of the dinosaurs lived. The periods are named after different bands of sedimentary rock, each of which has a distinctive collection of fossils.

▶ 23–2 MYA

Neogene
Mammals and birds evolved into recognizably modern forms in the Neogene. Our ape ancestors left the trees and adapted to life in grasslands by walking on two legs.

Dryopithecus

▶ 2 MYA to present

Quaternary
Our ancestors evolved larger brains in this period and invented ever more ingenious tools to hunt, make fire, build homes, sew clothes, and farm the land.

Homo habilis

66–23 MYA ◀

Paleogene
The death of the giant dinosaurs allowed mammals to take their place. They evolved from small nocturnal creatures into a great diversity of land and sea animals, including giant herbivores such as *Uintatherium*, which evolved special adaptations for digesting huge quantities of plant food.

Uintatherium

▶ 145–66 MYA

Cretaceous
Dinosaurs of the Cretaceous included *Tyrannosaurus* and the plant-eating ceratopsians, which had distinctive horned faces, neck frills, and beaks. All dinosaurs except for a few birds perished in a mass extinction at the end of the period, along with many other prehistoric animals.

Triceratops

Ichthyornis

Magnolia

359–299 MYA ◀

Carboniferous
This period gets its name from the carbon deposits found in its rock as coal. Coal is the fossilized remains of lush rainforests that covered the land. These were home to giant millipedes, giant dragonfly-like insects, and early amphibians, which had evolved from Devonian fish.

Sigillaria

Meganeura

419–359 MYA ◀

Devonian
Fish ruled the seas in the Devonian, which is sometimes called the age of fish. The largest of them were placoderms – jawed fish with armour-plated bodies to protect them from their enemies' jaws.

Rolfosteus

▶ 485–444 MYA

Ordovician
Warm seas covered much of Earth in the Ordovician, submerging the continent that would later form North America. The oceans teemed with trilobites – large, woodlouse-shaped creatures that scuttled across the seabed or swam shrimp-like through the water. The first fish and starfish appeared, and simple plants probably began to colonize the land.

Trilobite fossils

▶ 444–419 MYA

Silurian
Coral reefs flourished in the Silurian, providing habitats for the first fish with bones and the first fish with powerful, biting jaws rather than sucking mouths. Land plants remained small but they began to acquire the tough, water-carrying veins that would later form wood and trigger the rise of trees.

Baragwanathia

Changing planet

If you were to travel back in time to the Mesozoic Era – the age of dinosaurs – Earth would seem like an alien world. The continents had different shapes, the climate was hotter, and strange prehistoric plants covered much of the land. Dinosaurs and their prehistoric relatives ruled this world for nearly 175 million years. The vast span of time is divided into three different periods, each with its own distinct animal and plant life: the Triassic, the Jurassic, and the Cretaceous.

252–201 million years ago

Coelophysis

Horsetail

Shonisaurus

Ginkgo

Moss

Placerias

Triassic world

At the start of the Triassic Period, the continents were joined in a single supercontinent called Pangaea. Its interior was desert, but the climate was wetter near the coast, allowing forests of ginkgo trees and giant horsetails to grow. The first dinosaurs – small, two-legged meat-eaters – appeared in the Triassic. They coexisted with stocky, tusked plant-eating animals such as *Placerias* – a relative of early mammals.

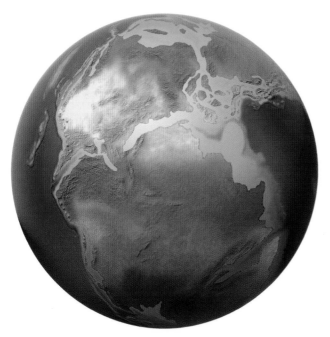

201–145 million years ago

145–66 million years ago

Jurassic world

The giant continent of Pangaea split during the Jurassic, torn apart by volcanic forces from deep inside Earth, and formed two large new continents. Moist sea air could now carry rain to more of the land, allowing forests to replace desert. Dinosaurs became the dominant land animals, and some evolved into giants, such as *Barapasaurus*, a long-necked plant-eater. The first feathered and flying dinosaurs evolved, including *Archaeopteryx*, a bird-like predator.

Archaeopteryx

Barapasaurus

Cycad

Fern

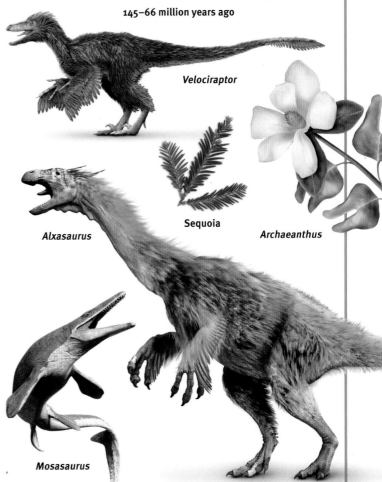

Velociraptor

Alxasaurus

Sequoia

Archaeanthus

Mosasaurus

Cretaceous world

During the Cretaceous the continents drifted towards their current configuration, moving about as fast as your toenails grow. Flowering plants evolved into trees and replaced older vegetation. There were now more kinds of dinosaur than ever, including *Velociraptor*, a small carnivore with lethal, hook-like claws on its hind feet, and *Alxasaurus*, a feathered herbivore.

11

Types of fossil

Most of what we know about prehistoric life comes from fossils – the remains of ancient organisms entombed in rock. The study of fossils and the sedimentary rocks containing them has enabled scientists to piece together a record of life on Earth.

Natural cast

Fossils can form in various ways. Some of the most common fossils are casts – replicas of a whole body or a body part that formed from minerals building up inside a cavity. This ammonite cast formed when minerals built up inside the animal's spiral shell after its soft inner tissues decayed.

Ammonite cast

How fossils form

Only a tiny fraction of the animals that lived in the past left fossils behind. Fossils of land animals are especially rare because they form only in unusual circumstances. The animal must die in a place where its body is undisturbed and scavengers can't easily consume it. Mud or sand needs to cover the remains, which must stay buried for millions of years as they slowly turn to rock. Geological forces must then bring the fossil back to the surface, where it can be found.

The body of a drowned Tyrannosaurus sinks to the muddy floor of a delta, where a river meets the sea.

Dinosaur drowns

The flesh slowly rots away, leaving behind hard body parts such as bones and teeth.

Flesh decays

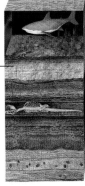

Thousands of years later, layers of mud and sand have buried the skeleton.

Sediment builds up

Trace fossil

Fossils that record an organism's activity – such as footprints, burrows, nests, or droppings – are known as trace fossils. Fossil footprints help us understand how animals moved.

Archosaur footprint

Mineralization

Most fossils involve a process called mineralization. Water seeping through the sediment dissolves remains such as bone and deposits crystallized rock minerals in their place, slowly turning the bones to rock.

This cast fossil replicates a trilobite's shape.

Mould

Mould fossils form in the same way as casts, but they preserve an imprint of the body rather than a replica of its shape. Trilobites were common sea creatures that grew by shedding their outer skeletons, leaving millions of fossils behind.

Trilobite mould

This mould fossil preserves an impression of a trilobite's body.

Petrified tree

Amber

A few fossils preserve the whole body of a prehistoric animal. Amber is a transparent yellow material formed from fossilized tree resin. It sometimes contains tiny animals that became trapped in the sticky resin as it oozed from a tree.

Prehistoric fly in amber

Petrification

Whole tree trunks can be fossilized by a process called petrification, which preserves minute details. First, groundwater seeping through buried wood deposits crystals of silica inside tiny spaces. Then, more slowly, minerals gradually replace the wood fibres, turning the trunk to stone.

Water seeping through the layers replaces the bones with rock minerals, turning the fossil to rock.

Bones turn to rock

Millions of years later, the continents have moved and the dinosaur fossil is no longer under the sea.

Continents move

Glaciers or other processes erode the ground, wearing away the sedimentary rock.

Erosion of surface

Erosion finally reveals the fossil, allowing paleontologists to excavate it.

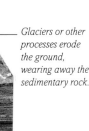

Discovery

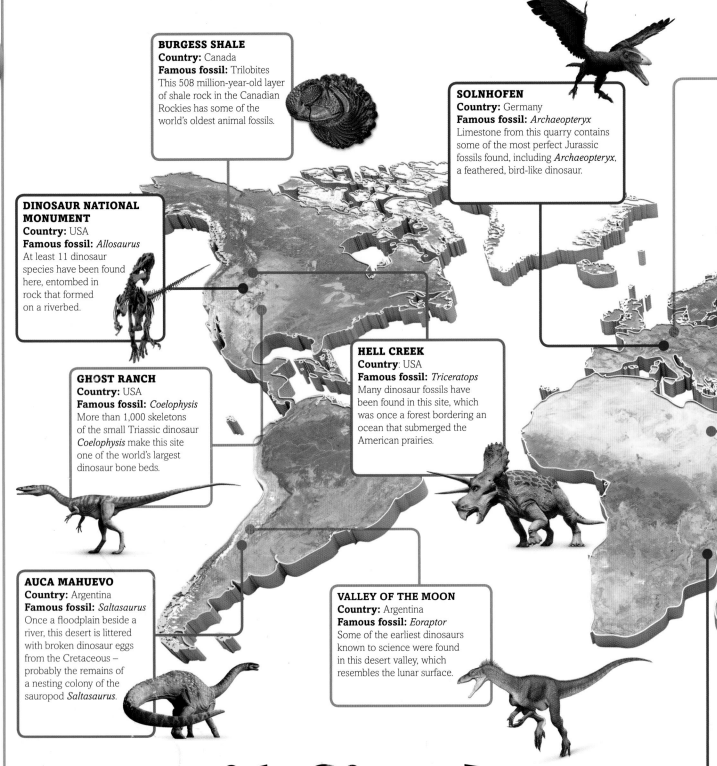

BURGESS SHALE
Country: Canada
Famous fossil: Trilobites
This 508 million-year-old layer of shale rock in the Canadian Rockies has some of the world's oldest animal fossils.

SOLNHOFEN
Country: Germany
Famous fossil: *Archaeopteryx*
Limestone from this quarry contains some of the most perfect Jurassic fossils found, including *Archaeopteryx*, a feathered, bird-like dinosaur.

DINOSAUR NATIONAL MONUMENT
Country: USA
Famous fossil: *Allosaurus*
At least 11 dinosaur species have been found here, entombed in rock that formed on a riverbed.

GHOST RANCH
Country: USA
Famous fossil: *Coelophysis*
More than 1,000 skeletons of the small Triassic dinosaur *Coelophysis* make this site one of the world's largest dinosaur bone beds.

HELL CREEK
Country: USA
Famous fossil: *Triceratops*
Many dinosaur fossils have been found in this site, which was once a forest bordering an ocean that submerged the American prairies.

AUCA MAHUEVO
Country: Argentina
Famous fossil: *Saltasaurus*
Once a floodplain beside a river, this desert is littered with broken dinosaur eggs from the Cretaceous – probably the remains of a nesting colony of the sauropod *Saltasaurus*.

VALLEY OF THE MOON
Country: Argentina
Famous fossil: *Eoraptor*
Some of the earliest dinosaurs known to science were found in this desert valley, which resembles the lunar surface.

Fossil finds

Most fossils are found in sedimentary rock that formed from ancient layers of mud and sand. Sedimentary rock is found worldwide, but a few key sites have especially clear fossils of animals that didn't fully decay, preserving fine details like feathers or skin. Many fossils are found in deserts, not because animals fossilize well in deserts but because the large expanses of exposed rock make fossils easier to spot.

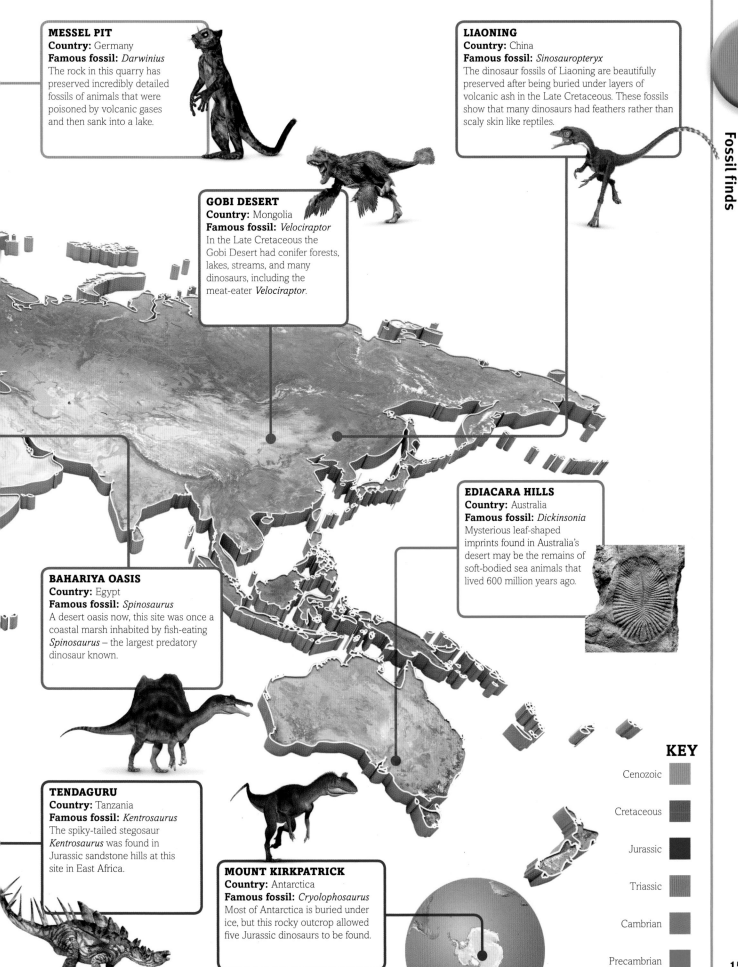

MESSEL PIT
Country: Germany
Famous fossil: *Darwinius*
The rock in this quarry has preserved incredibly detailed fossils of animals that were poisoned by volcanic gases and then sank into a lake.

LIAONING
Country: China
Famous fossil: *Sinosauropteryx*
The dinosaur fossils of Liaoning are beautifully preserved after being buried under layers of volcanic ash in the Late Cretaceous. These fossils show that many dinosaurs had feathers rather than scaly skin like reptiles.

GOBI DESERT
Country: Mongolia
Famous fossil: *Velociraptor*
In the Late Cretaceous the Gobi Desert had conifer forests, lakes, streams, and many dinosaurs, including the meat-eater *Velociraptor*.

EDIACARA HILLS
Country: Australia
Famous fossil: *Dickinsonia*
Mysterious leaf-shaped imprints found in Australia's desert may be the remains of soft-bodied sea animals that lived 600 million years ago.

BAHARIYA OASIS
Country: Egypt
Famous fossil: *Spinosaurus*
A desert oasis now, this site was once a coastal marsh inhabited by fish-eating *Spinosaurus* – the largest predatory dinosaur known.

TENDAGURU
Country: Tanzania
Famous fossil: *Kentrosaurus*
The spiky-tailed stegosaur *Kentrosaurus* was found in Jurassic sandstone hills at this site in East Africa.

MOUNT KIRKPATRICK
Country: Antarctica
Famous fossil: *Cryolophosaurus*
Most of Antarctica is buried under ice, but this rocky outcrop allowed five Jurassic dinosaurs to be found.

KEY

Cenozoic

Cretaceous

Jurassic

Triassic

Cambrian

Precambrian

15

Origin of life

Life on Earth began at least 3.5 billion years ago, and possibly more than 4 billion years ago. These oldest known life forms were microscopic single cells that lived in water – tiny capsules of watery fluid containing the complex chemicals vital to all types of life. How these cells formed is still not known, but the process was probably fuelled by the heat and chemical energy of hot springs, either on land or on the deep ocean floor.

Early Earth

Planet Earth was formed from the rock and dust that orbited the newly formed Sun. As the planet grew in size, its gravity attracted more rocks and comets, which contained water and the chemical elements needed for life. All the rocks impacting the growing planet made it heat up until it melted. Later, the planet cooled enough for liquid water to settle on the surface. Even today, liquid water is vital to all forms of life.

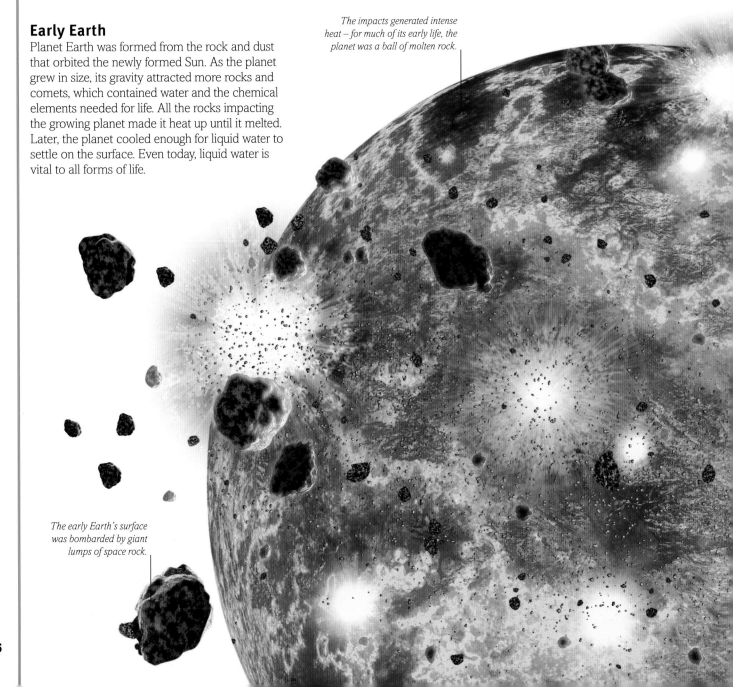

The impacts generated intense heat – for much of its early life, the planet was a ball of molten rock.

The early Earth's surface was bombarded by giant lumps of space rock.

First life

The first living organisms must have formed in water containing simple chemicals dissolved from rocks. Today, this type of chemical-rich water erupts from hot springs on the ocean floor and in places like Yellowstone National Park, USA. The water contains microscopic organisms that resemble some of the earliest living things, so it is likely that life began in such places. It is this microbial life that gives Grand Prismatic Spring its vibrant colours.

Grand Prismatic Spring, Yellowstone National Park, USA

The hot spring is fringed with microbial life.

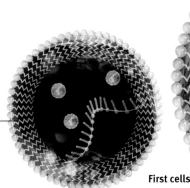

Tiny, tough-walled bubbles were the first living cells.

First cells

Living cells

Life involves chemical reactions that occur in microscopic, tough-walled containers called cells. The earliest living cells were simple bags of fluid, like modern bacteria. They soaked up energy and used it to turn simple chemicals into complex substances vital to life, such as proteins. This helped them grow, multiply, and form large colonies like the ones that live around hot springs today.

Evidence of early life

The oldest-known rocks on Earth contain microscopic structures that have been identified as fossil Archaea – organisms similar to bacteria. The rocks, which formed on the ocean floor, are at least 3.8 billion years old. But much clearer evidence of early life exists in the form of fossil stromatolites. Dating from about 3.4 billion years ago, these were once colonies of microbes called cyanobacteria that built up in dome-shaped layers. These layers are clearly visible in the fossils.

Stromatolite fossil

GAME-CHANGERS
The shallow waters of Shark Bay in Western Australia support a life form that has existed on Earth for billions of years – stromatolites. These muddy-looking lumps have been built up by cyanobacteria – simple microbes that turn air and water into sugar using sunlight. This process of photosynthesis creates most of the food that animals need, and releases the oxygen they breathe.

When cyanobacteria evolved in the oceans more than
2.5 billion years ago, there was very little oxygen in the air.
Over millions of years, they pumped out so much that it now
makes up more than a fifth of the atmosphere. This was vital
for the evolution of animals, which need oxygen to turn food
into energy. So all the animals that have ever lived owe their
existence to these microbes. Free-living cyanobacteria
are still widespread in oceans and on land, but thriving
stromatolites are rare because they were ideal food for some
of the animals that evolved in the world they had created.
The ones in Shark Bay survive because few animals can live
in the very salty water of its lagoons.

Evolution and extinction

Fossils reveal how life has changed over time. This was not fully understood until the 19th century, when fossils became important evidence supporting the theory of evolution by natural selection. Developed primarily by English scientist Charles Darwin, this theory showed that the individuals in a species vary in their ability to cope with the hardships of life – some survive and breed, while others do not. As a result, species gradually change over time as they adapt to the changing world. New species evolve, and older ones may die out completely, becoming extinct.

Fossil evidence

When the first fossil of *Archaeopteryx* showing wing feathers was discovered in 1861, it was seen as powerful evidence in favour of the theory that living things evolve over time.

Bony tail ❯ At first sight, this 150-million-year old fossil of an *Archaeopteryx* looks very like a living bird with broad, feathered wings. But it had a long, bony tail like an extinct dinosaur. This combination of features does not exist in any modern animal.

Natural selection

Every animal is different from its parents. This natural variation produces individuals with different strengths and weaknesses, so some are more likely to survive. An insect with more effective camouflage than its cousins will be more likely to evade hungry birds, breed, and pass on its advantages to its young, Meanwhile, its less well camouflaged relatives may die out.

The jagged edges and pattern of lines add to the leaf insect's superb camouflage.

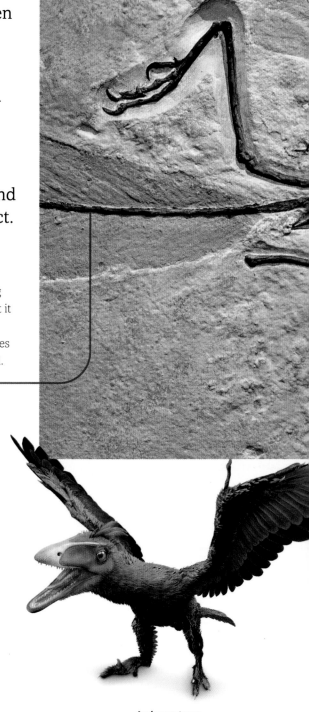

Leaf insect

Archaeopteryx

New species

If birds fly to a new habitat, such as an oceanic island, they may face difficulties in finding food. Those that survive will be the ones that, by some stroke of luck, have features that help them cope with the new conditions. If they manage to breed, their young will tend to inherit these features. Over many generations, this may give rise to an island form that is clearly different from its mainland ancestors. This process creates new species.

Wing feathers ❯ The fossils of *Archaeopteryx* preserve traces of feathers that are very similar to those of modern birds. But the fossils also show that it had the teeth and bones of a theropod dinosaur.

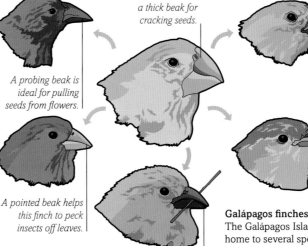

The ancestor had a thick beak for cracking seeds.

This finch uses its hooked beak to slice through fruit and buds.

A probing beak is ideal for pulling seeds from flowers.

A beak with an overbite is perfect for digging up grubs.

A pointed beak helps this finch to peck insects off leaves.

A tool-holding beak enables this finch to use a twig to dig out prey from bark.

Galápagos finches
The Galápagos Islands in the Pacific Ocean are home to several species of finch, each with a beak specialized for a different type of food. It is clear that they all evolved from the same ancestor, which probably arrived from nearby South America.

***Archaeopteryx* fossil**

Lost ancestors

The processes of evolution and extinction cause a relentless turnover of species, with new ones evolving as others die out. This means that, over the past 500 million years, more than 90 per cent of all species on Earth have vanished. We only know about these life forms because their remains have survived as fossils.

Trilobites don't exist today – they flourished in ancient seas about 500 years ago.

Trilobite fossil

Mass extinctions

Sometimes a catastrophic event changes the world so radically that very few animals can survive it. This is called a mass extinction. Since life began there have been five major mass extinctions. Each one wiped out much of the life on Earth at the time, allowing new species to evolve and take over.

ORDOVICIAN (444 MYA)
Up to 60 per cent of marine species perished in a mass extinction at the end of the Ordovician Period.

60%

DEVONIAN (359 MYA)
The Late Devonian extinction mainly affected oceanic life, especially in shallow coastal seas.

75%

PERMIAN (252 MYA)
The Permian Period ended with a global catastrophe that almost wiped out all life on Earth.

96%

TRIASSIC (201 MYA)
Many of the animals that coexisted with early dinosaurs died out at the end of the Triassic Period.

70%

CRETACEOUS (66 MYA)
This mass extinction destroyed the pterosaurs, giant dinosaurs, and most of the marine reptiles.

75%

The vertebrates

Vertebrae ❯ Vertebrates get their name from a chain of bones called vertebrae that form the neck, backbone, and tail.

Shoulder blade

Until about 530 million years ago, all animals were invertebrates – creatures with no internal jointed skeletons. But then new types of animal appeared in the oceans, with bodies strengthened by a springy rod – the beginnings of a backbone. These evolved into fish – the first true vertebrates and the ancestors of amphibians, mammals, reptiles, and birds.

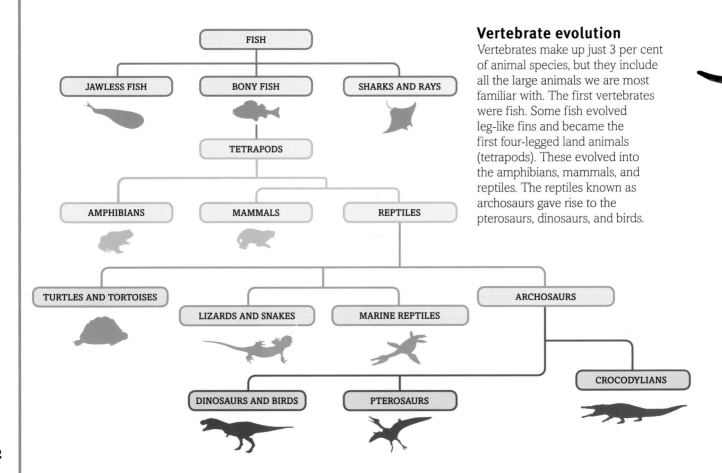

FISH

JAWLESS FISH

BONY FISH

SHARKS AND RAYS

TETRAPODS

AMPHIBIANS

MAMMALS

REPTILES

TURTLES AND TORTOISES

LIZARDS AND SNAKES

MARINE REPTILES

ARCHOSAURS

DINOSAURS AND BIRDS

PTEROSAURS

CROCODYLIANS

Vertebrate evolution

Vertebrates make up just 3 per cent of animal species, but they include all the large animals we are most familiar with. The first vertebrates were fish. Some fish evolved leg-like fins and became the first four-legged land animals (tetrapods). These evolved into the amphibians, mammals, and reptiles. The reptiles known as archosaurs gave rise to the pterosaurs, dinosaurs, and birds.

*Upper
hip bone*

*Spines jutting from the
top of the vertebrae
provided anchor points
for the back muscles.*

Framework ❯ The backbone between
the shoulders and hips supported this
plant-eater's head, neck, and tail as
well as the ribs. The backbone was
made up of interlocking bones that
were light but strong.

Leg bones ❯ The immense
weight of this giant dinosaur
was supported by massive leg
bones, linked to the backbone
by strong, mobile joints.

Diplodocus

All large land animals are vertebrates,
because a heavy land animal needs a
sturdy internal skeleton to support its
weight. During the age of giant dinosaurs,
strong bones enabled land animals like
Diplodocus to grow to colossal size. The
only animals that weigh more are whales,
but their weight is supported by the water.

Archosaur

Reptile

Mammal

Fish

Amphibian

Types of vertebrate

We usually think of the vertebrates as fish, amphibians,
reptiles, birds, and mammals. But the birds can also be
seen as the most successful and diverse living group of
archosaurs, a branch of the reptiles that also included
their closest relatives – the extinct dinosaurs.

What is a dinosaur?

Dinosaurs were a diverse and successful group of reptiles that dominated life on land for about 140 million years. Humans, for comparison, have existed for less than 1 million years. Ranging in size from animals no bigger than pigeons to lumbering giants the size of trucks, they were reptiles, but very different from modern reptiles. Dinosaurs can be split into two groups: lizard-hipped dinosaurs (saurischians) and bird-hipped dinosaurs (ornithischians). These can be split further, as shown.

Saurischians
Saurischian ("lizard hipped") refers to the typical saurischians that had hip bones like those of lizards. This group included the sauropodomorph plant-eaters. It may also have included the meat-eating theropods, but some scientists think that theropods are more closely allied to ornithischians.

Eoraptor

Ancestral dinosaurs
The first dinosaurs were small, agile animals that ran on two legs – they would have looked like this *Marasuchus*, an early, dinosaur-like archosaur. During the Late Triassic Period early dinosaurs evolved in different ways. Most became specialized for eating plants, but some were to become dedicated hunters.

Marasuchus

Ornithischians
This group is made up of beaked plant-eaters with relatively short necks. The name means "bird hipped", because their hip bones resembled those of birds (even though birds were small saurischians and so not closely related).

Hypsilophodon

Giraffatitan

Sauropodomorphs
The sauropodomorphs are named after the sauropods – giant, long-necked plant-eaters that did not have beaks and walked on four legs.

Ceratopsians
Most ceratopsians had horned heads and big bony frills extending from the back of their skulls. They were plant-eaters with hooked, parrot-like beaks.

Einiosaurus

Alioramus

Theropods
Theropods were nearly all meat-eaters that walked on two legs. Some were huge, powerful hunters, but the theropods also include birds.

Pachycephalosaurs
These dinosaurs had very thick skulls. They walked on two legs and probably ate a variety of plant and animal food.

Pachycephalosaurus

Marginocephalians

Ornithopods
The ornithopods were a group of beaked plant-eaters that mostly walked on two feet, but the biggest ones supported some of their weight on their hands.

Iguanodon

Stegosaurs
These beaked, plant-eating dinosaurs had rows of tall plates and spikes extending down their backs and tails. They all walked on four legs.

Stegosaurus

Ankylosaurs
Sometimes called tank dinosaurs, these plant-eating heavyweights had thick body armour for defence against large theropod predators.

Ankylosaurus

Thyreophorans

Inside a dinosaur

Although soft tissues of animals' bodies seldom fossilize, we can still figure out what dinosaurs were like on the inside. Dinosaurs were vertebrates, and all vertebrates share the same basic body plan, with powerful muscles connected to a jointed skeleton and internal organs that included a heart, lungs, stomach, intestines, and brain. Dinosaurs were once thought to be cold-blooded, lumbering reptiles, but we now think that many were as quick-witted and active as birds, and some may even have been warm-blooded.

Backbone

Tail muscle

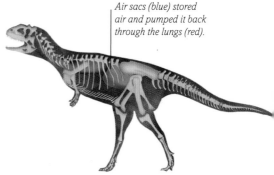

Tyrannosaurus

Leg muscles ❯ Big dinosaurs like this *Tyrannosaurus* had huge muscles. Heat generated inside the dinosaur's body kept the muscles warm, for maximum efficiency.

Thigh muscle

Dinosaur features

The brain of a dinosaur like Citipati *was adapted for sharp senses, not intelligence.*

The closest living relatives of extinct dinosaurs have four-chambered hearts.

Air sacs (blue) stored air and pumped it back through the lungs (red).

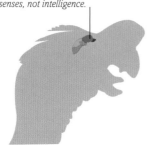

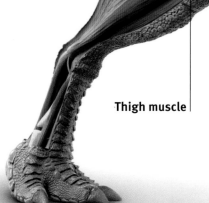

Brain The brains of extinct dinosaurs were relatively small, and some were tiny. Most would not have been as intelligent as modern birds.

Heart Pumping blood around the body of a giant dinosaur required a powerful four-chambered heart – similar to a bird heart, but a lot bigger.

Lungs Fossil evidence shows that most dinosaurs had lungs like those of modern birds, which are more efficient than the lungs of mammals.

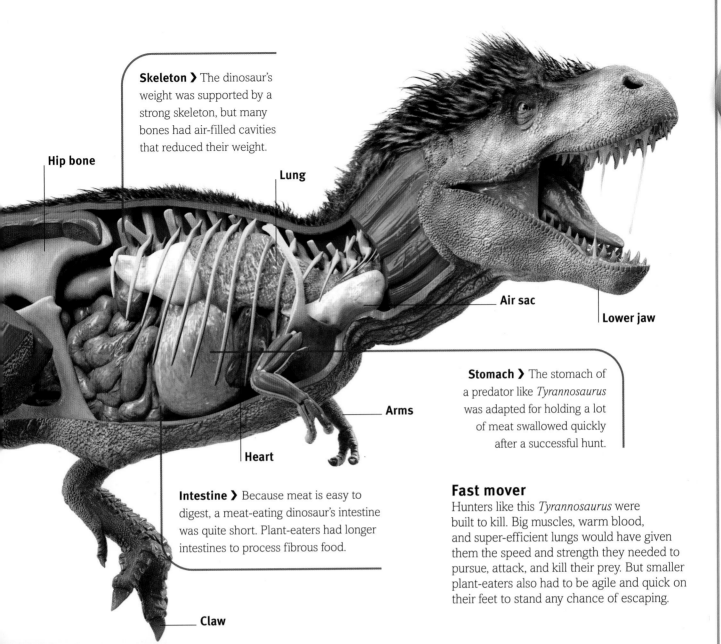

Skeleton ❯ The dinosaur's weight was supported by a strong skeleton, but many bones had air-filled cavities that reduced their weight.

Hip bone

Lung

Air sac

Lower jaw

Arms

Stomach ❯ The stomach of a predator like *Tyrannosaurus* was adapted for holding a lot of meat swallowed quickly after a successful hunt.

Heart

Intestine ❯ Because meat is easy to digest, a meat-eating dinosaur's intestine was quite short. Plant-eaters had longer intestines to process fibrous food.

Fast mover

Hunters like this *Tyrannosaurus* were built to kill. Big muscles, warm blood, and super-efficient lungs would have given them the speed and strength they needed to pursue, attack, and kill their prey. But smaller plant-eaters also had to be agile and quick on their feet to stand any chance of escaping.

Claw

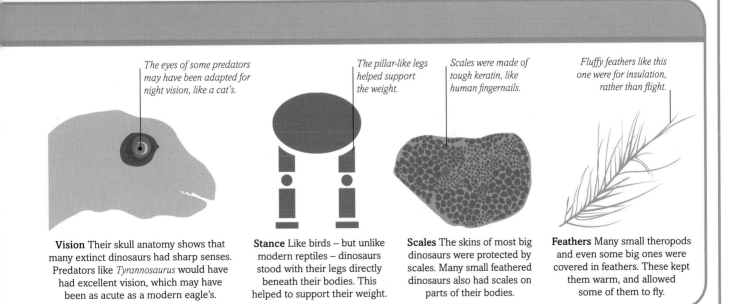

The eyes of some predators may have been adapted for night vision, like a cat's.

The pillar-like legs helped support the weight.

Scales were made of tough keratin, like human fingernails.

Fluffy feathers like this one were for insulation, rather than flight.

Vision Their skull anatomy shows that many extinct dinosaurs had sharp senses. Predators like *Tyrannosaurus* would have had excellent vision, which may have been as acute as a modern eagle's.

Stance Like birds – but unlike modern reptiles – dinosaurs stood with their legs directly beneath their bodies. This helped to support their weight.

Scales The skins of most big dinosaurs were protected by scales. Many small feathered dinosaurs also had scales on parts of their bodies.

Feathers Many small theropods and even some big ones were covered in feathers. These kept them warm, and allowed some of them to fly.

BEFORE THE DINOSAURS

The first animals

Best known from finds in Russia, Australia, and Namibia, this fossil of a worm-like animal has no evidence of a mouth, eyes, or even a gut.

Pteridinium

Charnia

Fossils show that Charnia's *body was made of rows of branches, giving it a striped appearance.*

Attached to the seabed by a stalk, Charnia *had a leaf-shaped body that absorbed food from the water.*

The flower-like fossils of Mawsonites *may be the remains of free-swimming jellyfish.*

Mawsonites

Scientists once thought that the first animals evolved about 541 million years ago at the start of the Cambrian Period. The huge span of Earth history before this, known as the Precambrian Period, was thought to be almost lifeless apart from bacteria and similar microscopic single-celled organisms. But in 1957 a fossil was discovered in the Precambrian rocks of Charnwood Forest in England. It was a multicelled life form, now known as ***Charnia***. Scientists then realized that fossils of similar organisms found in the

The head may have had eyes and a mouth.

Spriggina

Tribrachidium

Tribrachidium *resembled a sea anemone and had a circular body that was made up of three similar parts.*

The body was divided into many segments, but it had no obvious legs.

The largest known fossils of Dickinsonia *are more than 1.3 m (4 ft) long and show a distinctive body with a central groove, but no one knows if it even had a head.*

The first known Precambrian fossil, **Charnia**, was found by a 15-year-old schoolboy.

Dickinsonia

Ediacara Hills of Australia in 1946 were also Precambrian, and more than 600 million years old. These were some of the first animals on Earth. Since then, similar fossils have been found in North America, Africa, and Russia. Many, including *Charnia*, were animals that lived rooted on the seabed, like modern corals. Others, like **Spriggina**, were free-living animals that could roam or swim in search of food, and some, including **Dickinsonia**, were so unlike any modern animal that their nature and way of life are still a mystery.

Built to survive

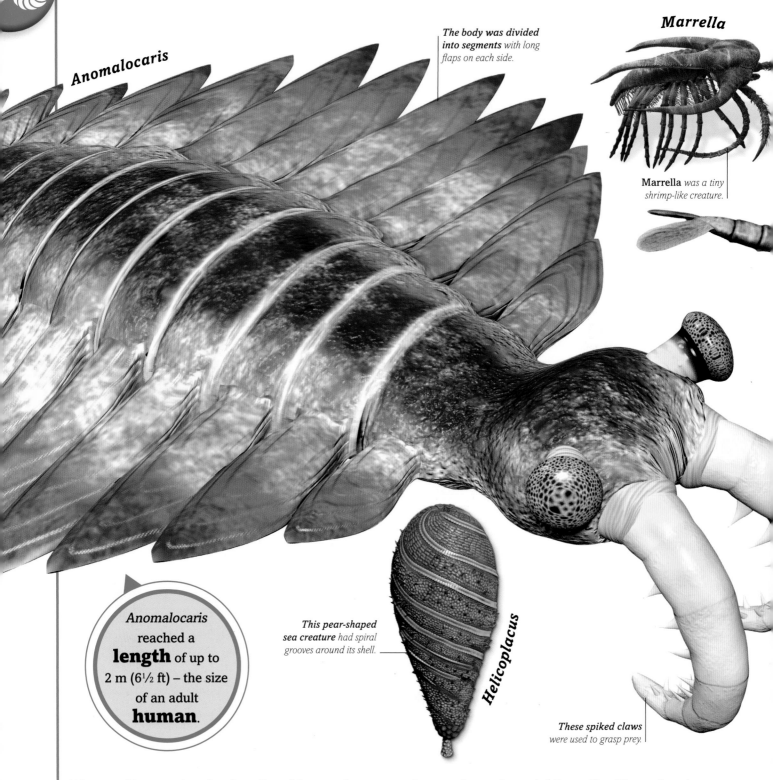

Anomalocaris

The body was divided into segments with long flaps on each side.

Marrella

Marrella *was a tiny shrimp-like creature.*

Anomalocaris reached a **length** of up to 2 m (6½ ft) – the size of an adult **human**.

This pear-shaped sea creature had spiral grooves around its shell.

Helicoplacus

These spiked claws were used to grasp prey.

The earliest animals that lived in ancient oceans had soft bodies, like modern jellyfish. But during the Cambrian Period, from 541 million years ago, new types of animals appeared. They had hard shells, spines, and tough external skeletons, such as those of

Anomalocaris and *Marrella*. These hard parts supported their bodies and helped protect them from enemies. When the animals died, their soft parts were eaten or rotted, but their shells and skeletons were often preserved as fossils. The appearance of many fossils in

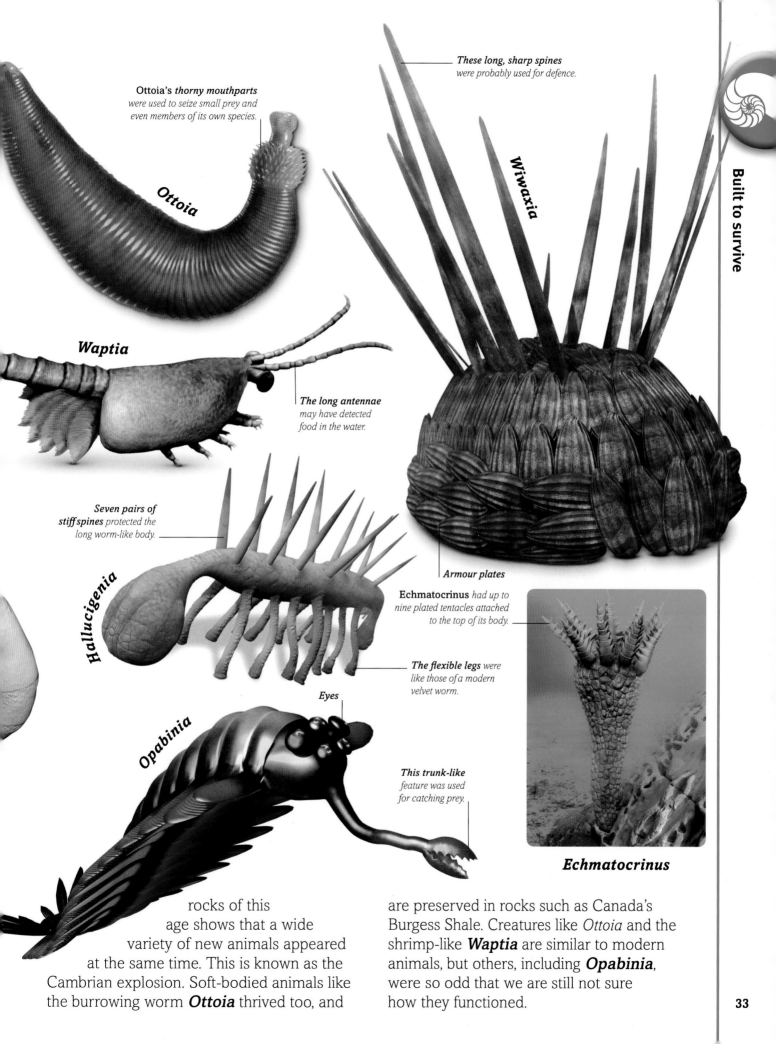

*Ottoia's **thorny mouthparts*** *were used to seize small prey and even members of its own species.*

Ottoia

These long, sharp spines were probably used for defence.

Wiwaxia

Waptia

The long antennae may have detected food in the water.

*Seven pairs of **stiff spines** protected the long worm-like body.*

Hallucigenia

Armour plates

Echmatocrinus had up to nine plated tentacles attached to the top of its body.

The flexible legs were like those of a modern velvet worm.

Opabinia

Eyes

This trunk-like feature was used for catching prey.

Echmatocrinus

rocks of this age shows that a wide variety of new animals appeared at the same time. This is known as the Cambrian explosion. Soft-bodied animals like the burrowing worm **Ottoia** thrived too, and are preserved in rocks such as Canada's Burgess Shale. Creatures like *Ottoia* and the shrimp-like **Waptia** are similar to modern animals, but others, including **Opabinia**, were so odd that we are still not sure how they functioned.

SET IN STONE
High in the Rocky Mountains of British Columbia, Canada, lies one of the most incredible fossil sites – the Burgess Shale. It was discovered in 1909 by American fossil hunter and scientist Charles Walcott, who realized he had stumbled upon a treasure trove of ancient life. He was to spend much of the next 14 years working on the site, splitting the rock to reveal over 65,000 fossils.

More than 500 million years ago, the Burgess Shale was a muddy seabed at the foot of a coastal cliff. The water teemed with animals, some of which were buried by mudslides. As the mud turned to rock, their remains were preserved as flattened fossils, recording the variety of life that had evolved by the start of the Paleozoic Era, about 541 million years ago.

Some of the fossils were of animals that had exoskeletons, such as these trilobites, but many more were of soft-bodied animals that were very different from the creatures we see today, such as the five-eyed *Opabinia*. These animals provide scientists with a spectacular snapshot of life millions of years ago.

Trilobites

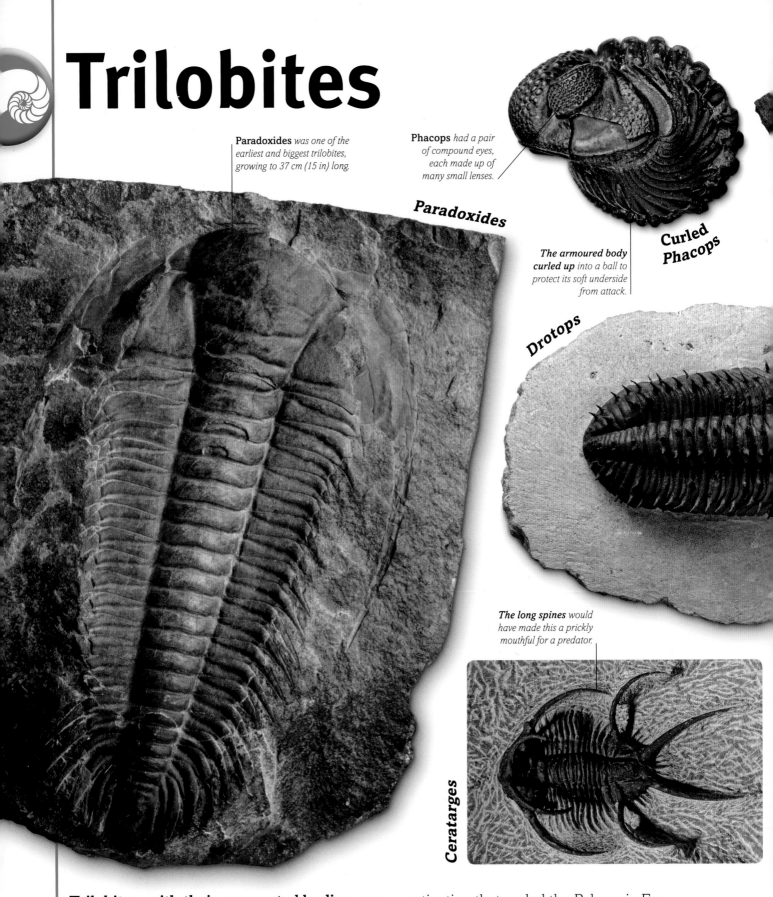

Paradoxides *was one of the earliest and biggest trilobites, growing to 37 cm (15 in) long.*

Phacops *had a pair of compound eyes, each made up of many small lenses.*

Paradoxides

Curled Phacops

*The armoured body **curled up** into a ball to protect its soft underside from attack.*

Drotops

The long spines would have made this a prickly mouthful for a predator.

Ceratarges

Trilobites, with their segmented bodies, are among the most distinctive fossils found in ancient rocks. The earliest trilobites appear in rocks that are more than 520 million years old. They thrived in the oceans for an amazing 270 million years until the catastrophic mass extinction that ended the Paleozoic Era 252 million years ago. Trilobites were some of the earliest arthropods – animals with external skeletons and jointed legs, like today's insects and spiders. Many trilobites like **Drotops** looked like flattened woodlice, with several pairs of legs

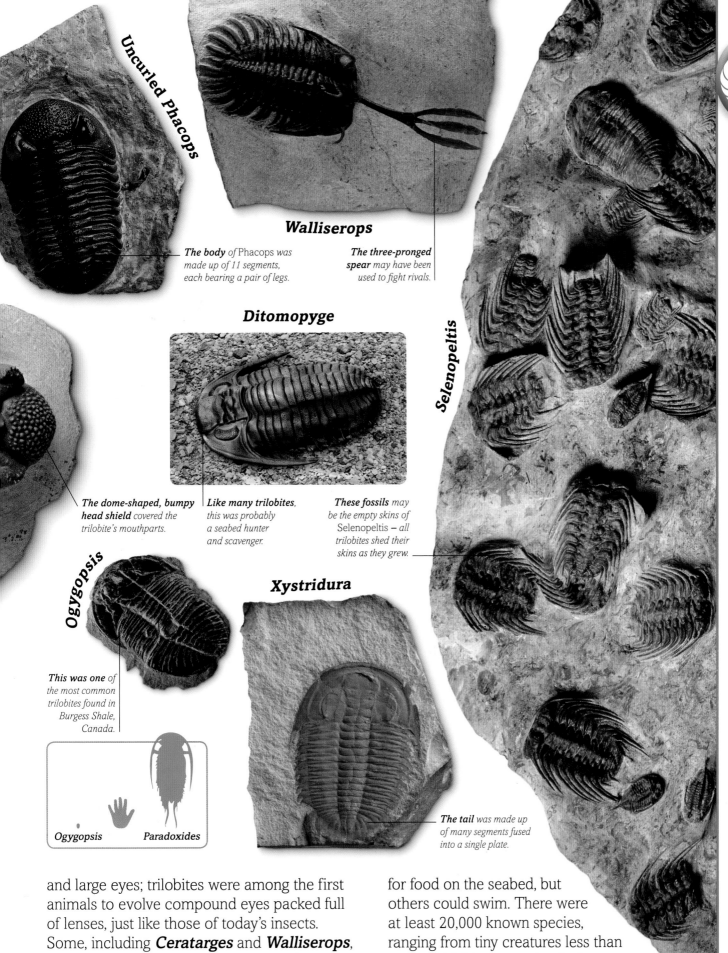

Uncurled Phacops

Walliserops

Ditomopyge

Selenopeltis

Xystridura

Ogygopsis

The body of Phacops was made up of 11 segments, each bearing a pair of legs.

The three-pronged spear may have been used to fight rivals.

The dome-shaped, bumpy head shield covered the trilobite's mouthparts.

Like many trilobites, this was probably a seabed hunter and scavenger.

These fossils may be the empty skins of Selenopeltis – all trilobites shed their skins as they grew.

This was one of the most common trilobites found in Burgess Shale, Canada.

Ogygopsis   Paradoxides

The tail was made up of many segments fused into a single plate.

and large eyes; trilobites were among the first animals to evolve compound eyes packed full of lenses, just like those of today's insects. Some, including **Ceratarges** and **Walliserops**, had spectacular spines that may have been for courtship or defence. Many would have foraged for food on the seabed, but others could swim. There were at least 20,000 known species, ranging from tiny creatures less than 3 mm (⅛ in) long to animals that were as big as this book.

37

The age of fish

The long spine projecting from the head may have been venomous for defence.

With its elongated body, this late Paleozoic shark looked more like an eel.

Cheirolepis

Xenacanthus

This bony fish had a shark-like tail.

The backbone extended into the upper lobe of the tail, as in modern sharks.

Stethacanthus

The body was covered in tiny, diamond-shaped scales.

Astraspis

A long, flexible **"whip"** trailed from each side fin.

The fins of this spiny shark were supported by stout spines.

The head of this primitive jawless fish was protected by scaly armour.

Cheiracanthus

All land vertebrates, including dinosaurs, are descended from fish – the first animals to have backbones. Fish evolved from soft-bodied creatures like **Pikaia**, which lived more than 500 million years ago. Early forms like **Astraspis** had a soft, jawless mouth and a flexible rod called a notochord in place of a bony spine. Over the next 100 million years, fish developed hinged jaws and backbones. During the Devonian Period, 419–359 million years ago, they became so successful that this period is known as the age of fish. Two main groups

Unlike modern sharks, the mouth was at the tip of the snout, rather than on the underside.

Cladoselache

Pikaia was a primitive chordate – an animal with a spinal cord, but no bones.

Pikaia

The strange flat-topped **structure** on the back of males may have been used to attract a female.

A long, flat body extended from behind Pikaia's small head.

Stethacanthus had **many tooth-like scales** on its head and dorsal fin.

This armoured fish had a bony head shield.

Coccosteus fossil

The shark's sleek, streamlined body was adapted for fast movement through the water.

Large scales covered the body of this lobe-finned fish.

Holoptychius

The paired fins under the body contained strong limb bones.

evolved – sharks like **Stethacanthus** and **Cladoselache** had skeletons made of a rubbery material called cartilage, while the so-called bony fish like **Cheirolepis** had skeletons of hardened bone. Some of these fish also had four stout, bony fins beneath their bodies. Called the lobe-finned fish, they were the first vertebrates to crawl out of the sea and live on land. Fish have continued to flourish ever since; even though the largest mass extinction wiped out 90 per cent of marine species 252 million years ago, fish managed to survive.

Fish armour

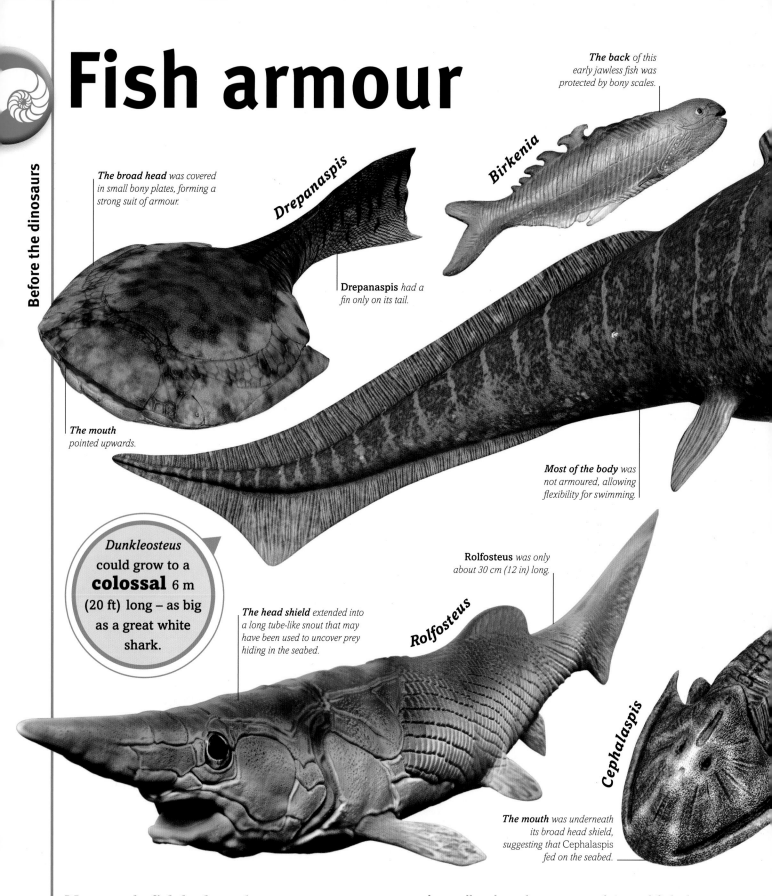

The back of this early jawless fish was protected by bony scales.

Birkenia

The broad head was covered in small bony plates, forming a strong suit of armour.

Drepanaspis

Drepanaspis *had a fin only on its tail.*

The mouth pointed upwards.

Most of the body was not armoured, allowing flexibility for swimming.

Dunkleosteus could grow to a **colossal** 6 m (20 ft) long – as big as a great white shark.

Rolfosteus *was only about 30 cm (12 in) long.*

The head shield extended into a long tube-like snout that may have been used to uncover prey hiding in the seabed.

Rolfosteus

Cephalaspis

The mouth was underneath its broad head shield, suggesting that Cephalaspis fed on the seabed.

Many early fish had tough armour protecting their heads, and sometimes their bodies too. The first of these armoured fish appeared more than 400 million years ago. The jawless **Cephalaspis** and **Drepanaspis** had big horseshoe-shaped head shields. They were much smaller than the armoured, jawed fish that evolved later – the placoderms. Some of these massive jawed fish were monstrous looking. Their heads and upper bodies were covered with tough, overlapping plates of bone that were hinged to allow movement. The armour

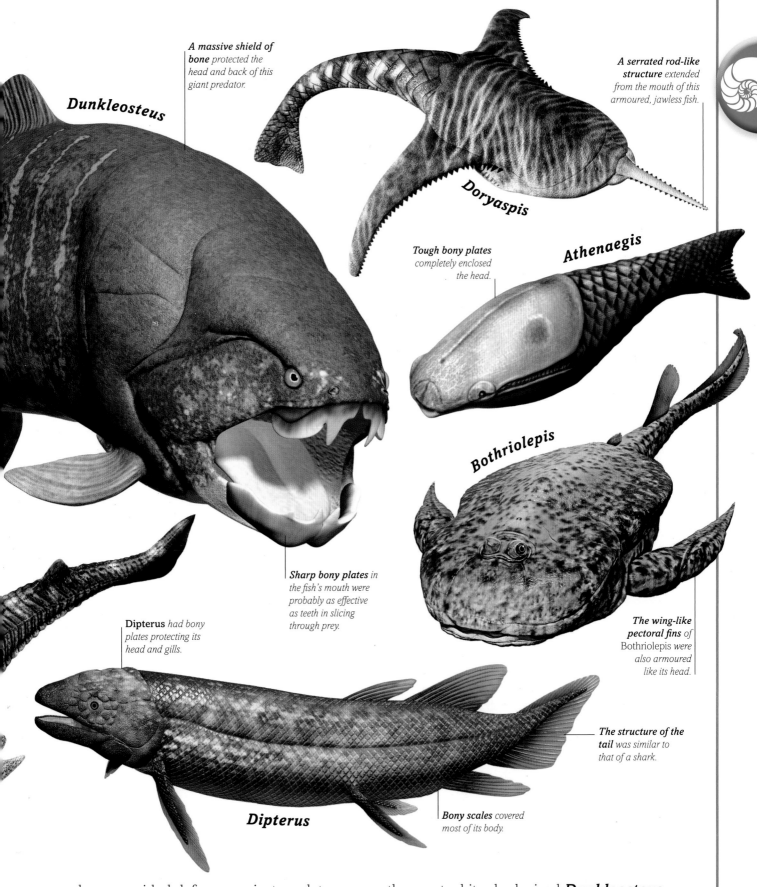

Dunkleosteus

A massive shield of bone protected the head and back of this giant predator.

A serrated rod-like structure extended from the mouth of this armoured, jawless fish.

Doryaspis

Tough bony plates completely enclosed the head.

Athenaegis

Bothriolepis

Sharp bony plates in the fish's mouth were probably as effective as teeth in slicing through prey.

The wing-like pectoral fins of Bothriolepis were also armoured like its head.

Dipterus had bony plates protecting its head and gills.

The structure of the tail was similar to that of a shark.

Bony scales covered most of its body.

Dipterus

may have provided defence against predators. The only animals that might threaten them were sharks and other big, fish-eating predators, since the fearsome marine reptiles with their powerful jaws did not appear in the oceans for another 100 million years. Some of the placoderms, like the great white shark-sized **Dunkleosteus** would have had few enemies – it had one of the most powerful bites of any fish and bony plates that were about 5 cm (2 in) thick. It is also likely that they were armoured as defence against each other.

Early life on land

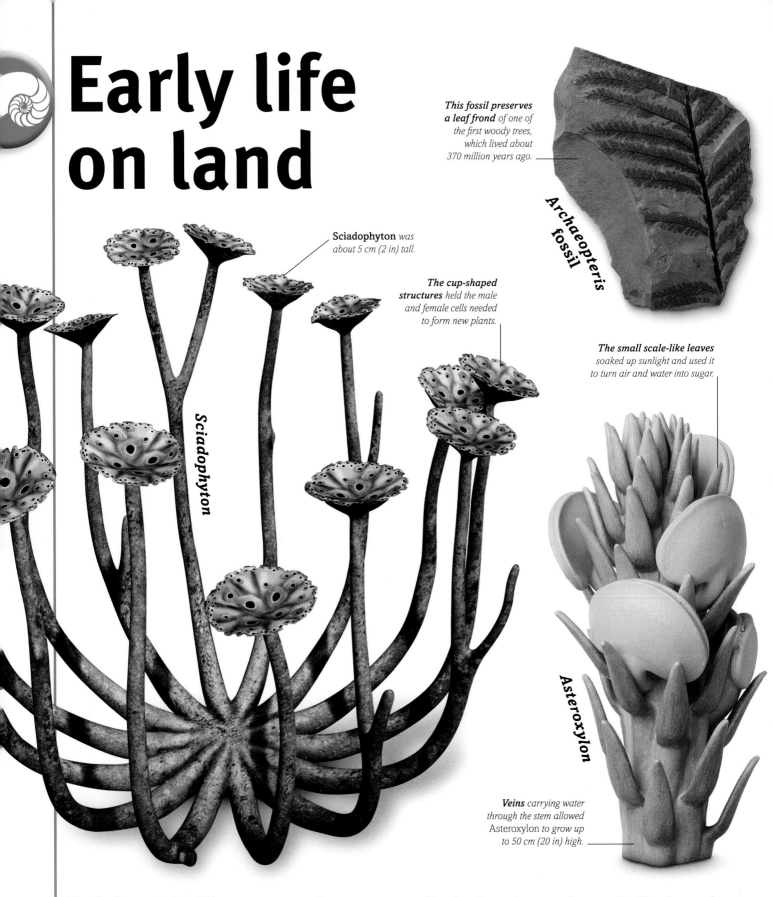

This fossil preserves **a leaf frond** of one of the first woody trees, which lived about 370 million years ago.

Archaeopteris fossil

Sciadophyton was about 5 cm (2 in) tall.

The cup-shaped structures held the male and female cells needed to form new plants.

The small scale-like leaves soaked up sunlight and used it to turn air and water into sugar.

Sciadophyton

Asteroxylon

Veins carrying water through the stem allowed Asteroxylon to grow up to 50 cm (20 in) high.

Until about 500 million years ago, there was no life on land. The continents were barren rock and sand like the surface of Mars. The first land organisms were probably microscopic bacteria that built up in mats. These were followed by fungi that lived off the bacterial mats and broke them down to form soil, allowing early plants to get a root-hold. Spores of these plants have been found in fossils that formed about 476 million years ago. The plants would have looked like **Aglaophyton** and **Sciadophyton** – simple, moss-like plants that grew close to the

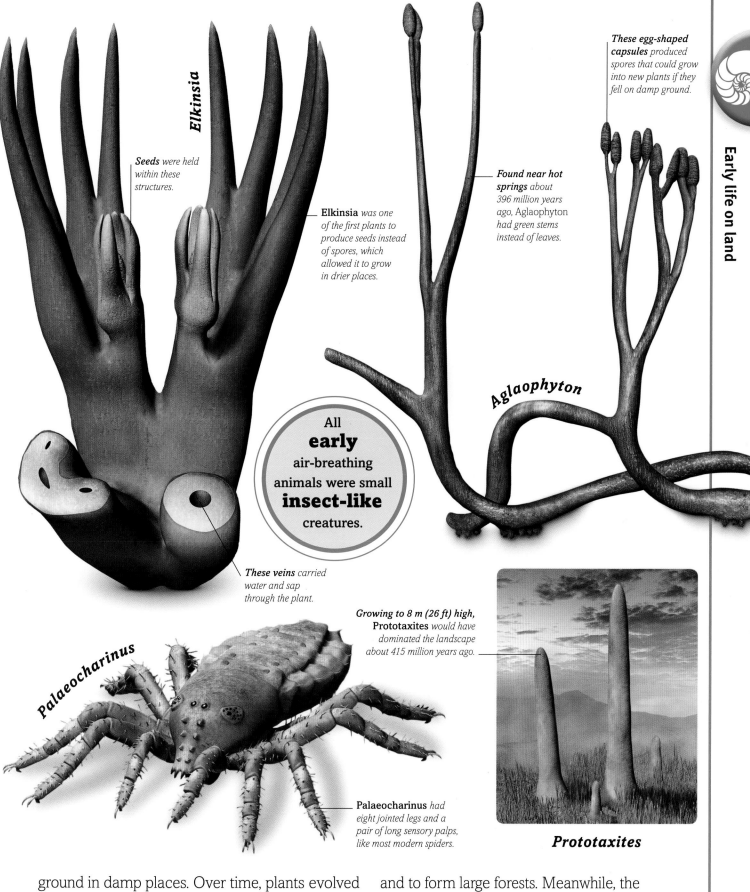

Elkinsia

Seeds were held within these structures.

Elkinsia was one of the first plants to produce seeds instead of spores, which allowed it to grow in drier places.

These egg-shaped capsules produced spores that could grow into new plants if they fell on damp ground.

Found near hot springs about 396 million years ago, Aglaophyton had green stems instead of leaves.

Aglaophyton

All **early** air-breathing animals were small **insect-like** creatures.

These veins carried water and sap through the plant.

Palaeocharinus

Growing to 8 m (26 ft) high, Prototaxites would have dominated the landscape about 415 million years ago.

Palaeocharinus had eight jointed legs and a pair of long sensory palps, like most modern spiders.

Prototaxites

ground in damp places. Over time, plants evolved veins that allowed water and sap to flow through stems connecting their roots and leaves. This allowed them to grow taller, eventually leading to trees like the 6 m (20 ft) high **Archaeopteris** – the first tree to have dense wood and true leaves,

and to form large forests. Meanwhile, the fungi, bacteria, and plants provided food for early land animals like the millipede *Pneumodesmus*. These small animals were in turn hunted by predators, including the spider-like **Palaeocharinus**.

Towering trees

*This fossilized **leaflet** had a heart-shaped base.*

Macroneuropteris

This early conifer had a tall, straight trunk and short, needle-shaped leaves.

Lepidodendron

The bark of this giant clubmoss had a distinctive diamond pattern.

Walchia

Despite its fern-like leaves, Alethopteris produced seeds instead of spores.

Alethopteris

Alethopteris   Lepidodendron

Although known as the age of fish, the Devonian Period also saw the transformation of land habitats by plant life. The first woody trees appeared in the Late Devonian, about 385 million years ago, and spread to form the earliest forests. During the next 85 million years,

throughout the Carboniferous Period, trees and other plants colonized the land and created habitats for animal life. Many of these plants grew in swamps, and when they died, their remains formed peat that ultimately turned to coal. Some trees, such

Paripteris seed

Paripteris leaf

Ferns like Paripteris were some of the first plants to evolve seeds.

Shed leaves left scars that formed a honeycomb-like pattern on the bark.

This primitive plant resembled a tree fern.

Glossopteris once formed **lush forests** on the continent of **Antarctica**.

Sigillaria

Wattieza

Glossopteris *means "tongue fern" describing its leaf shape.*

The fossilized leaves were very like modern fern fronds.

Glossopteris

Neuropteris leaves

as **Sigillaria** and **Lepidodendron**, looked similar to modern trees but were clubmosses – relatives of mosses and ferns. These could grow to great heights – *Lepidodendron* towered 40 m (130 ft) or more. Many plants resembled modern spore-bearing ferns and horsetails, but others, including **Alethopteris** and **Paripteris**, bore true seeds. By the Late Carboniferous, plants like **Walchia** had evolved – the first of the pine-like conifer trees that later became an important food source for dinosaurs.

Arthropod empire

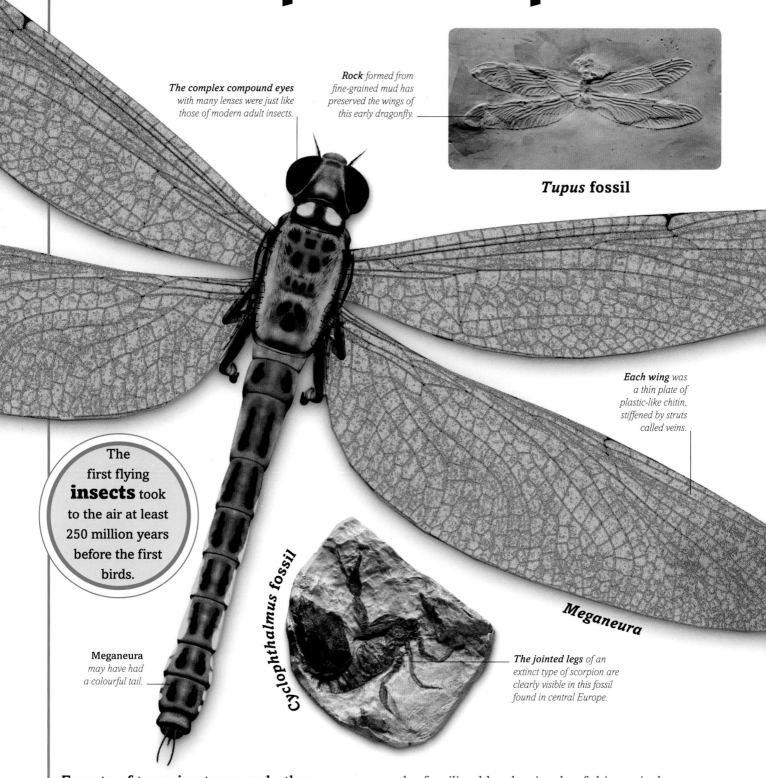

The complex compound eyes with many lenses were just like those of modern adult insects.

Rock formed from fine-grained mud has preserved the wings of this early dragonfly.

***Tupus* fossil**

Each wing was a thin plate of plastic-like chitin, stiffened by struts called veins.

The first flying **insects** took to the air at least 250 million years before the first birds.

Cyclophthalmus fossil

Meganeura

Meganeura *may have had a colourful tail.*

The jointed legs of an extinct type of scorpion are clearly visible in this fossil found in central Europe.

Forests of towering trees and other plants spread over the land from about 359–299 million years ago, providing food for many small plant-eating animals. They included soft-bodied animals like worms, whose burrows have been found fossilized. But most of the fossilized land animals of this period were arthropods – creatures with tough external skeletons and jointed legs, like today's insects, spiders, and crustaceans. They included early millipedes like **Euphoberia**, and plant-eating insects like **Archimylacris** – a type of

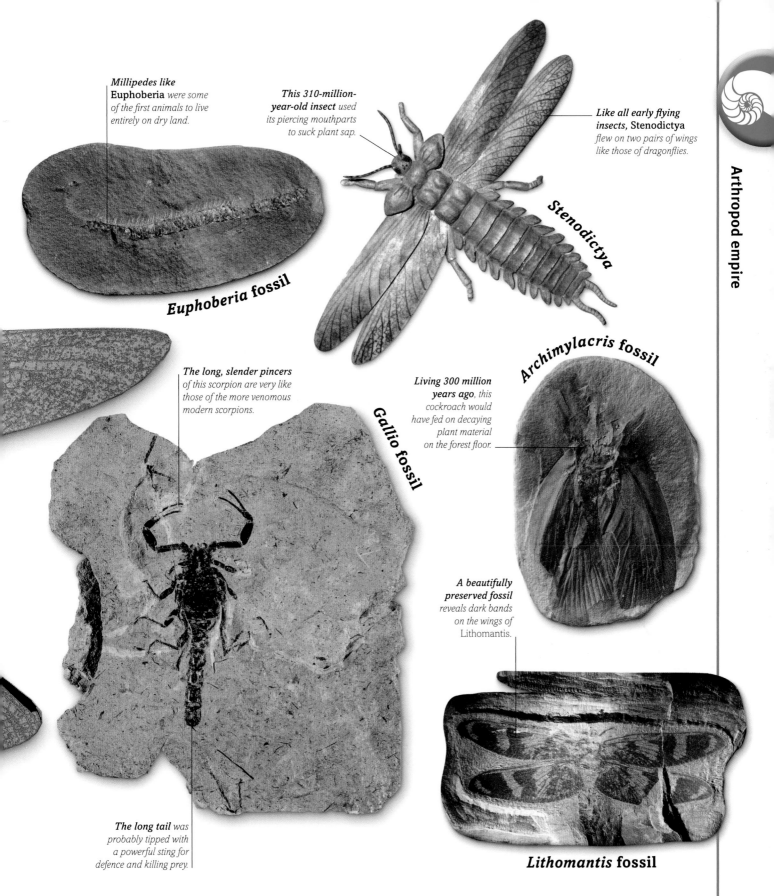

Millipedes like **Euphoberia** *were some of the first animals to live entirely on dry land.*

This 310-million-year-old insect used its piercing mouthparts to suck plant sap.

Like all early flying insects, **Stenodictya** *flew on two pairs of wings like those of dragonflies.*

Euphoberia fossil

Stenodictya

Archimylacris fossil

The long, slender pincers of this scorpion are very like those of the more venomous modern scorpions.

Living 300 million years ago, this cockroach would have fed on decaying plant material on the forest floor.

Gallio fossil

A beautifully preserved fossil reveals dark bands on the wings of Lithomantis.

The long tail was probably tipped with a powerful sting for defence and killing prey.

Lithomantis fossil

cockroach. They were hunted by predatory centipedes, early spiders, scorpions like **Cyclophthalmus**, and insects like **Meganeura**. The forests would have been buzzing with these animals, especially insects that, in an era before birds, were the only animals able to fly. Many would have spent most of their lives as wingless nymphs or grubs that lived underwater or in the ground, before emerging as winged adults. Like modern mayflies, these may have had very short adult lives, but they have survived for millions of years as fossils.

AIRBORNE GIANT
Some of the most spectacular insects that ever lived flew through the lush forests of the Carboniferous Period, about 300 million years ago. They were griffinflies – extinct relatives of modern dragonflies, but far bigger. Fossils of the largest known dragonfly relative, *Meganeura*, show that its wingspan reached more than 69 cm (27 in), almost four times the size of the biggest living dragonflies.

Like its modern counterparts, *Meganeura* was a hunter that preyed on other insects. It probably used the same predatory technique, targeting airborne prey and seizing them with its bristly legs. Flying back to a perch, *Meganeura* would then use its powerful biting jaws to chew through its prey's tough armour to reach the soft flesh within. *Meganeura* would have laid its eggs in water, and after these hatched, the young would live underwater for several years before emerging to change into adult, flying insects. The puzzle about *Meganeura* is how it could grow so much bigger than any living dragonfly. One theory is that higher oxygen levels in the atmosphere allowed insects to grow larger than they do now.

Early amphibians

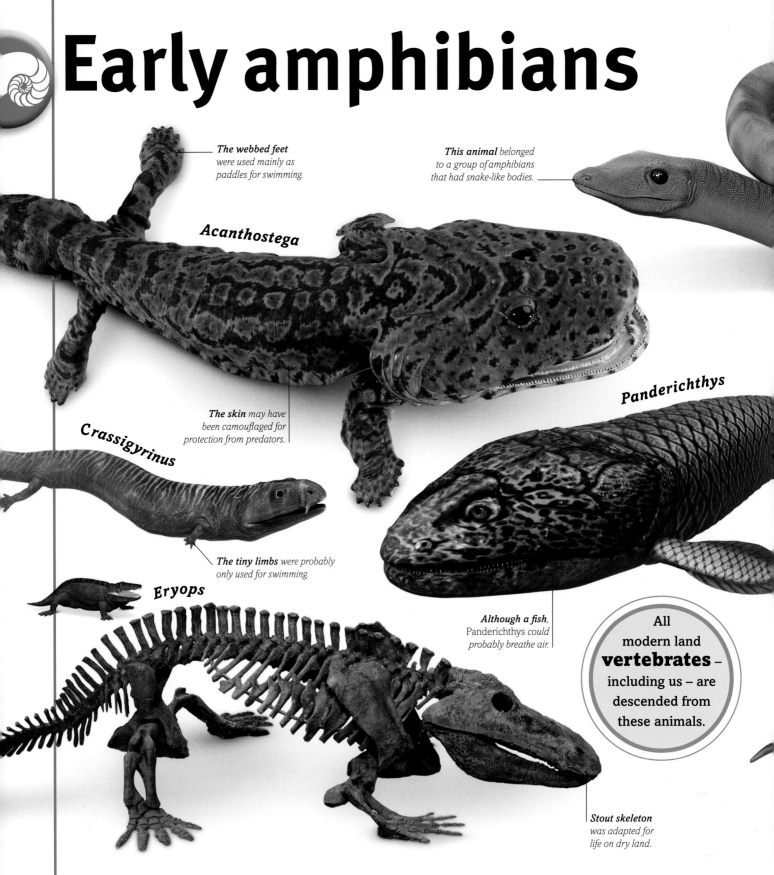

The webbed feet were used mainly as paddles for swimming.

This animal belonged to a group of amphibians that had snake-like bodies.

Acanthostega

The skin may have been camouflaged for protection from predators.

Crassigyrinus

Panderichthys

The tiny limbs were probably only used for swimming.

Eryops

Although a fish, Panderichthys *could probably breathe air.*

All modern land **vertebrates** – including us – are descended from these animals.

Stout skeleton was adapted for life on dry land.

The first four-legged animals on land were amphibians, much like our modern frogs and salamanders. Their ancestors were Devonian fish like **Panderichthys** and **Eusthenopteron**, which had unusually stout bones supporting the four fins beneath their bodies. Some of these fish, the immediate ancestors of tetrapods, evolved to survive out of the water by using their lungs and mouths for breathing. **Acanthostega** and **Tiktaalik** may have lived at least partly on land. By about 359 million years ago, amphibians

Phlegethontia

Tiktaalik

The strong bony fins were to evolve into legs.

Seymouria fossil

Seymouria's *skull* was unusually thick and strong.

The body was protected by big scales.

Powerful tail propelled this fish through water.

Eusthenopteron

Amphibamus

Long front and hind limbs were the same size.

such as **Amphibamus** had developed proper feet, but they still had to keep their skin moist to survive. They also had to return to the water to lay their eggs, because the eggs of all amphibians are like those of fish, and dry up if they are not laid in wet places. Eventually, amphibians similar to **Eryops** and **Seymouria** evolved into a group of animals that were better adapted to live on dry land – the first reptiles.

51

Rise of the reptiles

Mesosaurus

Proterogyrinus

This aquatic animal lived like an amphibian, but had developed reptile-like eggs.

Tough bony plates helped protect this plant-eater from predators.

Scutosaurus

The broad, strong skull was probably adapted for burrowing.

Westlothiana is named after **West Lothian** in Scotland, where its fossils were **found**.

Procolophon

Stout, pillar-like legs supported the animal high off the ground.

The slender body and short legs may have been an adaptation for burrowing.

Scales stopped vital body moisture escaping easily through the skin.

Early amphibians could live on land, but they lost body moisture through their thin skin, and had to lay their eggs in water or damp places if they were to survive. During the Carboniferous Period, some amphibian-like animals resembling **Proterogyrinus** and

Westlothiana evolved eggs enclosed in shells that retained moisture, so they could be laid in dry places. They also developed thicker skin covered with tough, waterproof scales that stopped the body losing moisture. They were the ancestors of the first true reptiles – animals such

Spinoaequalis

Spinoaequalis *lived in water but was only partly aquatic – it returned to dry land to breed.*

The feet *were well suited to life on land.*

Hyperodapedon

The plant-eating Hyperodapedon *had a razor-sharp beak.*

Like modern crocodiles, Mesosaurus *hunted in the water.*

Westlothiana

Stagonolepis

Distantly related to the ancestors of dinosaurs, this armoured Triassic reptile ate a wide variety of food.

as ***Spinoaequalis*** and ***Mesosaurus***, which would ultimately give rise to lizards, snakes, and crocodiles. This new type of vertebrate was ideally equipped to colonize dry land during the Permian Period – an age of huge deserts that began 299 million years ago. Permian reptiles included a variety of plant-eaters like the armoured ***Scutosaurus*** as well as sharp-toothed hunters. Some survived the catastrophic mass extinction at the end of the Permian and became the ancestors of the dinosaurs.

Reptiles branch out

This synapsid had a barrel-shaped body.

Moschops

Slender and agile, Effigia *ran on two legs like a bird.*

Effigia

The sail was probably used for display, but may have also helped it to absorb or lose heat.

Dimetrodon

Placerias

Dimetrodon *had dagger-like canine teeth at the front for tearing into flesh, and numerous sharp-edged teeth at the back.*

The two big tusk-like canine teeth were probably used for digging.

Ophiacodon

The semi-aquatic Ophiacodon *could use its powerful limbs as paddles.*

Long before the first dinosaurs, about 320 million years ago, some reptiles evolved into animals known as synapsids – they would eventually give rise to the mammals. One of the earliest of these animals – **Ophiacodon** – had sprawling lizard-like limbs.

Some, including the predatory **Dimetrodon** and plant-eating **Edaphosaurus**, had huge "sails" on their backs supported by rod-like spine bones. Later, about 299 million years ago, these reptile-like animals gave rise to a group of animals called dicynodonts – **Placerias** was

Postosuchus *had a huge head.*

The armour of small bony plates protected its back.

The crocodile-like powerful jaws *were packed with sharp teeth.*

Archosaurs like **Postosuchus** preyed on early **dinosaurs**.

Postosuchus

Edaphosaurus

The jaws *of this plant-eating animal were lined with numerous blunt teeth.*

among the largest of these animals. A few similar animals survived the catastrophic mass extinction at the end of the Permian and evolved into cynodonts, which became the ancestors of modern mammals. Meanwhile, the reptile line had given rise to archosaurs – the group of animals that eventually included crocodylians, pterosaurs, dinosaurs, and birds. Some of the more powerful Triassic archosaurs, like **Postosuchus** were the top predators of their time. Others, including **Effigia**, were very similar in build to the first dinosaurs.

HUNGRY HUNTER
Concealed by its camouflaged scaly skin, which closely matches the surrounding ferns, a hungry, sail-backed *Arizonasaurus* stalks a herd of plant-eating dicynodonts – relatives of mammals. Reptiles like *Arizonasaurus* were the main threat to plant-eaters in the Middle Triassic Period, before the evolution of big predatory dinosaurs.

The first dinosaurs evolved during the Triassic Period, but they were not the giant, ruling reptiles that we are familiar with. The Triassic world was ruled by reptiles of a different type – animals like *Arizonasaurus*. They were archosaurs, as were the dinosaurs, but had evolved along different lines to resemble high-walking crocodiles. Many had massive jaws and teeth, and were capable of overpowering and eating any animal they might encounter. *Arizonasaurus* belonged to a group of archosaurs that had tall "sails" on their backs, supported by bones extending up from the spine. The function of the sail is uncertain, but it may have been important during displays to rival animals of the same species.

THE AGE OF DINOSAURS

The first dinosaurs

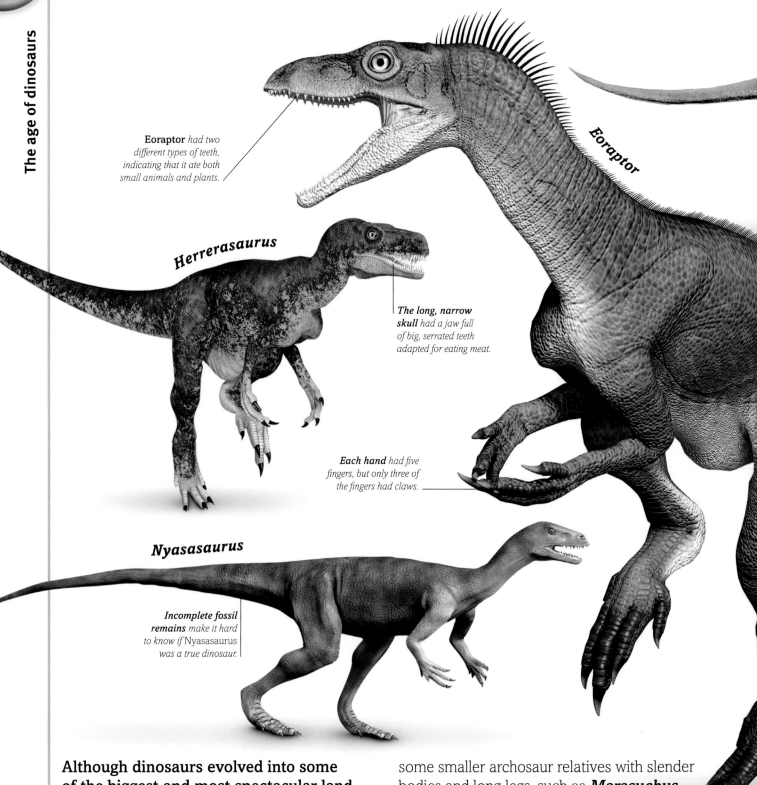

Eoraptor *had two different types of teeth, indicating that it ate both small animals and plants.*

Eoraptor

Herrerasaurus

The long, narrow skull had a jaw full of big, serrated teeth adapted for eating meat.

Each hand had five fingers, but only three of the fingers had claws.

Nyasasaurus

Incomplete fossil remains make it hard to know if Nyasasaurus was a true dinosaur.

Although dinosaurs evolved into some of the biggest and most spectacular land animals the world has seen, they had small beginnings. About 240 million years ago, in the Middle Triassic, the largest reptiles were powerful, crocodile-like archosaurs. These had

some smaller archosaur relatives with slender bodies and long legs, such as **Marasuchus**, which was just 70 cm (28 in) long and chased after small prey on its hind legs. The bigger, slightly more dinosaur-like **Silesaurus** had a similar build, but seems to have eaten plants

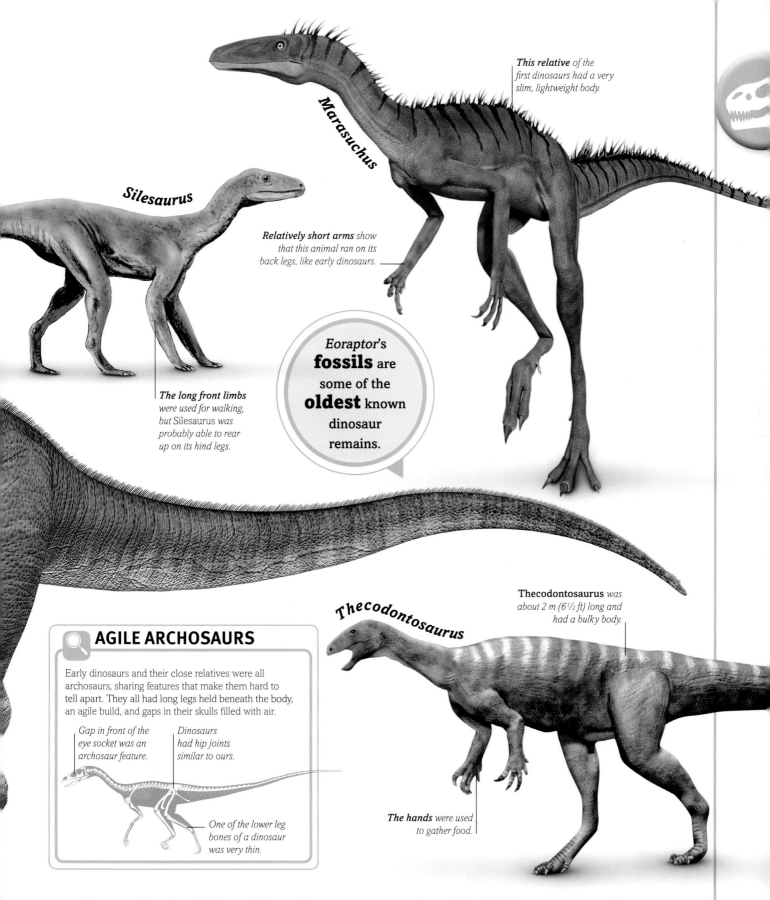

Marasuchus

This relative of the first dinosaurs had a very slim, lightweight body.

Relatively short arms show that this animal ran on its back legs, like early dinosaurs.

Silesaurus

The long front limbs were used for walking, but Silesaurus was probably able to rear up on its hind legs.

Eoraptor's **fossils** are some of the **oldest** known dinosaur remains.

Thecodontosaurus

Thecodontosaurus was about 2 m (6½ ft) long and had a bulky body.

The hands were used to gather food.

AGILE ARCHOSAURS

Early dinosaurs and their close relatives were all archosaurs, sharing features that make them hard to tell apart. They all had long legs held beneath the body, an agile build, and gaps in their skulls filled with air.

Gap in front of the eye socket was an archosaur feature.

Dinosaurs had hip joints similar to ours.

One of the lower leg bones of a dinosaur was very thin.

as well as small animals. These light, agile creatures were closely related to animals like **Nyasasaurus**, which may have been one of the first true dinosaurs. The first definite dinosaurs – animals like **Eoraptor** – lived about 230 million years ago and were probably omnivores that ate a variety of foods. They soon gave rise to specialized predators like **Herrerasaurus**, as well as plant-eaters like **Thecodontosaurus**. These animals were the ancestors of the giant dinosaurs that were to dominate life on land for the next 140 million years.

Prosauropods

Fossils of this giant prosauropod were found in La Rioja Province, Argentina.

Riojasaurus

Massospondylus

Set within its jaws were small, leaf-shaped teeth that had serrated edges to help slice through vegetation.

The long, flexible neck was well adapted for browsing on tree foliage.

The strong back legs supported all of the dinosaur's weight, leaving its hands free.

Seitaad

The remains of Seitaad, meaning "sand monster" in the Navajo language, were found near the Grand Canyon, USA.

A heavy tail balanced the dinosaur's body at the hips, enabling it to reach up into the trees easily.

Soon after the evolution of the first dinosaurs in the Middle Triassic (around 230–225 million years ago), dinosaurs began to diversify into species with different lifestyles. Some specialized in eating plants. They evolved long necks that helped them reach into trees, but their heads stayed relatively small. One of the earliest, **Saturnalia**, was only about 1.8 m (6 ft) long, but its relatives were to get a lot bigger; by the Late Triassic, **Riojasaurus** was about 10 m (33 ft) long and weighed as much as an elephant. These

Anchisaurus

At just 2 m (6½ ft) long, this slender, lightweight dinosaur was one of the smaller prosauropods.

Saturnalia   Riojasaurus

The skin may have been patterned for camouflage in the dappled shade of Triassic forests.

Found in China, this horse-sized prosauropod was a close relative of Massospondylus.

Plateosaurus

Strong hands could grip branches to pull them within reach of the dinosaur's jaws.

Lufengosaurus

Fossils of *Plateosaurus* have been found in more than **50 places** in Europe.

Saturnalia

Light and agile, Saturnalia would have run through the forest like a large wild turkey.

dinosaurs were the ancestors of the enormous sauropods, so they are known as prosauropods. They stood on two legs, balanced by their long tails, and used their shorter arms to gather food. **Plateosaurus** had grasping hands with four fingers and a powerful clawed thumb, which may also have been useful for defence. When it closed its jaws, its upper teeth overlapped the lower ones like scissor blades to slice through leaves. The tough, fibrous plant material was processed in a big digestive system to extract as much food value as possible.

63

Sauropods

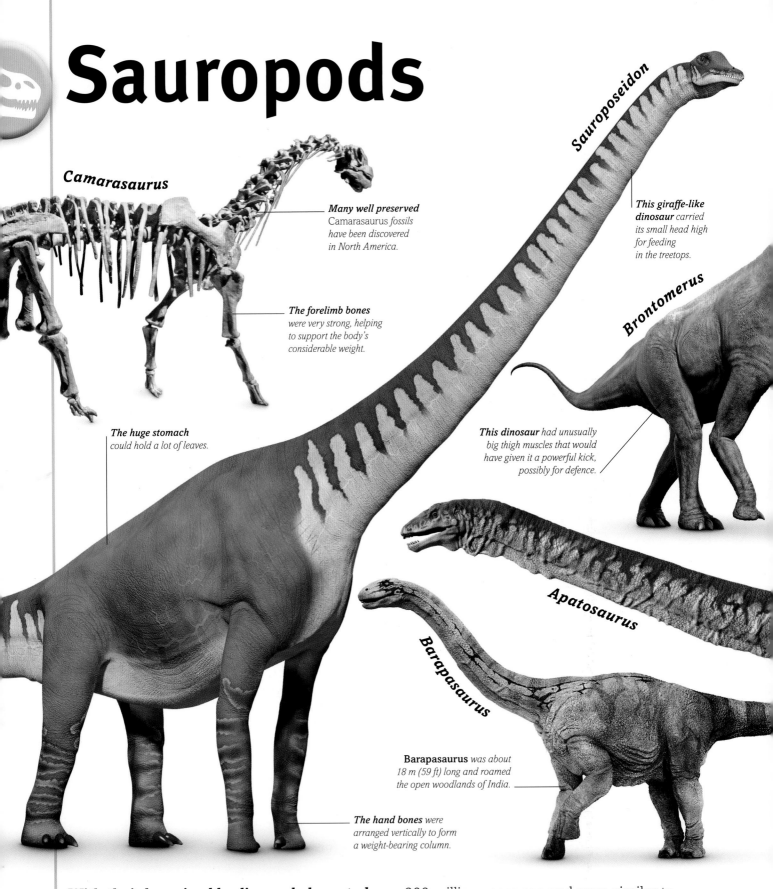

Camarasaurus

Many well preserved Camarasaurus *fossils have been discovered in North America.*

The forelimb bones *were very strong, helping to support the body's considerable weight.*

The huge stomach *could hold a lot of leaves.*

Sauroposeidon

This giraffe-like dinosaur *carried its small head high for feeding in the treetops.*

Brontomerus

This dinosaur *had unusually big thigh muscles that would have given it a powerful kick, possibly for defence.*

Apatosaurus

Barapasaurus

Barapasaurus *was about 18 m (59 ft) long and roamed the open woodlands of India.*

The hand bones *were arranged vertically to form a weight-bearing column.*

With their bus-sized bodies and elongated necks and tails, sauropods were the biggest dinosaurs ever to roam the Earth. These giants were plant-eaters; they would have browsed continually to fuel their enormous bodies. The earliest ones appeared about 200 million years ago and were similar to *Barapasaurus*. Unlike their prosauropod ancestors, they used their arms to support their bodies, and their hands became weight-bearing feet. Despite this, many could probably rear up on their hind legs to feed in the treetops. Others,

Brontomerus was a macronarian – a type of sauropod with a very big nose compared to its skull.

The immensely long neck spines were probably for display to rivals and breeding partners.

Hundreds of teeth lined the front of the distinctive shovel-shaped snout.

Nigersaurus usually held its neck high but could lower it to feed on small plants.

Amargasaurus

Giraffatitan

Nigersaurus

Spinophorosaurus

> Giraffatitan was **twice as tall** as a modern giraffe.

This sauropod had a spiked club at the end of its tail, possibly for defence or fights with rivals.

The forelimbs of Giraffatitan were unusually long, giving it a very high reach.

Apatosaurus had a very long, almost whip-like tail.

The massive feet had to support a lot of body weight, equivalent to four elephants.

Amargasaurus   *Sauroposeidon*

like **Sauroposeidon** and **Giraffatitan**, had long arms that helped raise their shoulders much higher than their hips, allowing them to reach the tallest trees without rearing up. The simple teeth of typical sauropods were adapted for biting or ripping leaves from trees, but not for chewing.

They swallowed the leaves and relied on their huge digestive systems to process them. A few sauropods like **Nigersaurus** had more complex teeth at the front of their wide snouts. These teeth may have been specialized for eating plants growing at ground level.

Mobile necks

Diplodocus

Diplodocus *had 15 neck bones – some were 1 m (3 ft) long.*

Mamenchisaurus
had 19 neck bones – the most of any known dinosaur.

Mamenchisaurus

Einiosaurus

The neck was just long enough to graze on low-growing plants.

Coelophysis

This dinosaur had a long, flexible neck.

Some dinosaurs – especially the plant-eating sauropods – had such astonishingly long necks that it is hard to imagine how they held their heads up. The neck of **Mamenchisaurus** could be up to 18 m (59 ft) long, which is eight times longer than the neck of a full-grown giraffe. Dinosaur neck bones, or vertebrae, were full of air cavities that made them light, enabling the animals to strip leaves from tall trees. Small, nimble

The neck bones of **Amargasaurus** *had bony spines that may have formed a spiky crest.*

Amargasaurus

Although Tyrannosaurus *had a short neck, it had powerful neck muscles that helped support the enormous head.*

Tyrannosaurus

Sauropods had the longest necks of any known animal.

Stegosaurus

The underside of the neck was protected by plates of bone hidden in the skin.

predators such as **Coelophysis** had S-shaped necks that they could straighten in an instant to snap up small prey. Big hunters like **Tyrannosaurus** had stout, massively powerful necks to support their huge skulls and jaws, and to give them the strength to tear prey apart. But most ornithischians, including **Stegosaurus** and **Einiosaurus**, had relatively short necks suitable for feeding on low-growing plants.

Titanosaurs

The very long neck of **Patagotitan** *enabled it either to gather leaves from treetops or reach down to feed near the ground.*

The teeth were probably spoon-shaped and quite small, suitable for biting through leaf stems.

About 30 m (98 ft) long, Dreadnoughtus was another gigantic animal with a big appetite. Its name means "fears nothing".

Dreadnoughtus

The body of this small, short-necked titanosaur was armoured with bony plates, each up to 12 cm (5 in) across.

Saltasaurus

Until quite recently, scientists thought that the giant sauropods had mostly died out by the end of the Jurassic Period, 145 million years ago. But since the 1980s, many sauropod fossils have been discovered showing that they lived on, and continued evolving until the very end of the age of dinosaurs. These late sauropods are known as titanosaurs. The name is misleading, because it suggests that they were all titanic giants. They were certainly big, and some of them were colossal – **Patagotitan**, for example, could turn

COLOSSAL GIANT

Found in 2008 in Patagonia, Argentina, the bones of *Patagotitan* are so big that its total length is estimated to be up to 37 m (121 ft), with a weight equivalent to 12 African elephants. Only the blue whale is heavier.

Titanosaurs had long tails, but not as long as the tails of many earlier sauropods.

This is one of the few titanosaurs that has been preserved with a fossil skull, so we know that it had a short snout.

Malawisaurus

Despite this animal's immense weight, it walked on the tips of its hand bones.

out to be the biggest land animal that ever lived. But other titanosaurs, including **Saltasaurus** and **Malawisaurus**, were no bigger than elephants, which is small by sauropod standards. Over the 80 million years of their existence, the titanosaurs evolved many different head shapes and body forms, suited to a wide variety of feeding habits and lifestyles. Despite this, they were all herbivores, specialized for devouring vast quantities of leaves and other plant material. Fossil evidence also suggests that they probably lived in herds and nested together.

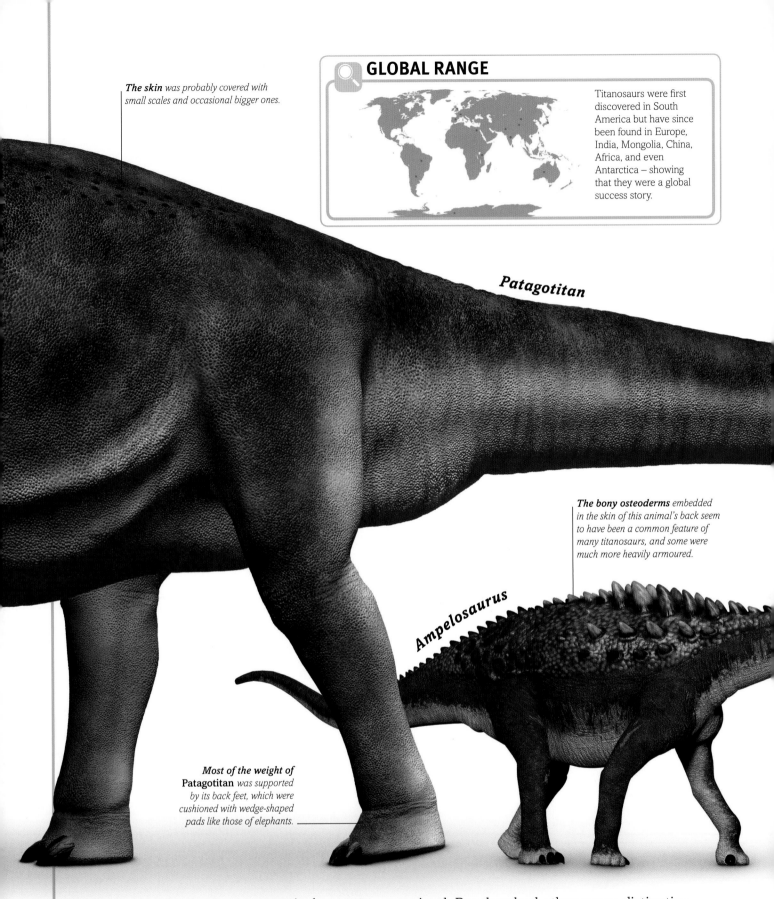

The skin was probably covered with small scales and occasional bigger ones.

Titanosaurs were first discovered in South America but have since been found in Europe, India, Mongolia, China, Africa, and even Antarctica – showing that they were a global success story.

Patagotitan

The bony osteoderms embedded in the skin of this animal's back seem to have been a common feature of many titanosaurs, and some were much more heavily armoured.

Ampelosaurus

Most of the weight of **Patagotitan** was supported by its back feet, which were cushioned with wedge-shaped pads like those of elephants.

In many ways, titanosaurs were typical sauropods, with long necks, long tails, and bulky bodies supported on all four limbs. In giants like **Patagotitan** and **Puertasaurus**, their length, bulk, and especially weight were close to the maximum possible for a land animal. But they had other, more distinctive features. Their hands were better adapted for bearing weight than those of earlier sauropods, and later titanosaurs like *Saltasaurus* and **Nemegtosaurus** had no finger bones; they stood on pillar-like structures made up of the

Saltasaurus   Patagotitan

Puertasaurus

With its **long** neck, *Puertasaurus* could reach **food** more than 15 m (49 ft) high.

The neck *of this giant titanosaur was up to 9 m (30 ft) long, and its total length may have been anything up to 30 m (98 ft).*

Nemegtosaurus

The skull *of this dinosaur has never been found, so scientists have had to base this reconstruction on the fossil remains of close relatives.*

Known from a single skull *found in the Gobi Desert of Mongolia, this titanosaur is 70 million years old, making it one of the last giant dinosaurs to walk the Earth.*

same bones that form the palms of our hands. Titanosaurs had unusually broad chests, and this meant that their forelimbs were spaced wide apart; trackways of fossilized titanosaur footprints are easy to recognize because the marks left by their feet are so widely spaced.

Many titanosaurs also had a feature not seen in earlier sauropods – body armour. The skin of **Ampelosaurus**, for example, was studded with tough bony plates and spikes called osteoderms, which would have helped protect it from the teeth of big predators.

Footprints and trackways

Found in Mongolia, **giant** footprints up to **2 m** (6½ ft) wide were made by titanosaurs.

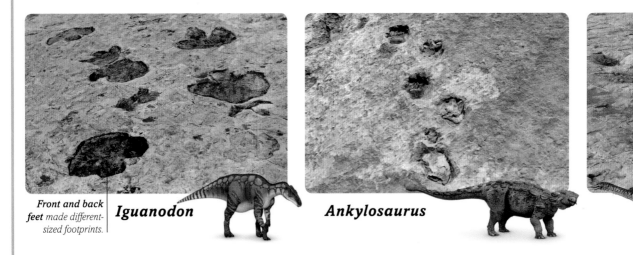

Front and back feet made different-sized footprints. **Iguanodon**

Ankylosaurus

Fossilized bones can tell us a lot about how the dinosaurs were built, but less about how they lived. Fossilized footprints, however, can show how dinosaurs walked and ran and whether they lived alone or in a group. A single footprint does not tell us much more than what type of animal made it; the most interesting information comes from trackways – sets of footprints left by animals on the move. The angle and spacing of the prints show how they placed their feet. The spacing also reveals the stride length, and if this varies it indicates

Titanosaur

STRIDE LENGTH

If we know how long a dinosaur's legs were, the length of its stride indicated by a line of footprints can show how fast it was moving. It may also show it speeding up or slowing down.

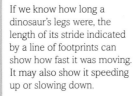

Running
Stride length 5.7 m (18½ ft)

Walking
Stride length 2.7 m (8¾ ft)

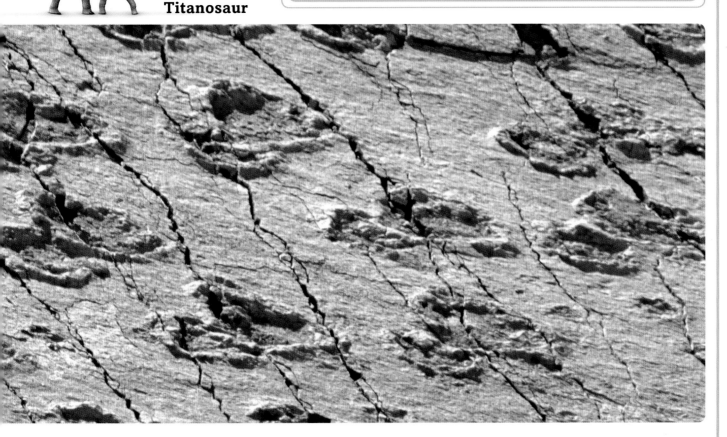

Apatosaurus

Coelophysis

Three-toed footprints are typical of theropod hunters.

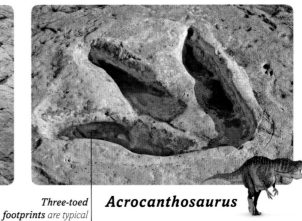

Acrocanthosaurus

a change of speed. Small and large footprints found together might have been left by a family, while a complex pattern of overlapping footprints could be evidence of a whole herd on the move. One 113-million-year-old trackway in Texas, USA, can even be read like a story, since it seems to show a big sauropod being stalked by a hunter – possibly the powerful theropod ***Acrocanthosaurus***. At one point the footprints converge, perhaps revealing the exact spot where the predator made its attack.

Stegosaurs

A medium-sized dinosaur, Loricatosaurus lived in Jurassic England and France.

Loricatosaurus

Dacentrurus

The flat, diamond-shaped plates were covered with a tough layer of skin.

Adratiklit

This dinosaur from North Africa is one of the oldest species of stegosaur.

At 4 m (13 ft) long, Huayangosaurus *was one of the smallest stegosaurs.*

Huayangosaurus

The front legs were shorter than the back legs, so the head was close to the ground.

With a double row of tall, pointed, bony plates running down its back and tail, *Stegosaurus* is one of the most instantly recognizable dinosaurs. But it was just one of many similar stegosaurs that lived during the Jurassic and Early Cretaceous Periods in various parts of the world – USA, Europe, India, China, and Africa. All stegosaurs bristled with plates and spikes along their backs, and many, such as the extra-spiky *Dacentrurus* and *Kentrosaurus*, also had spikes sprouting from their shoulders. These may have been

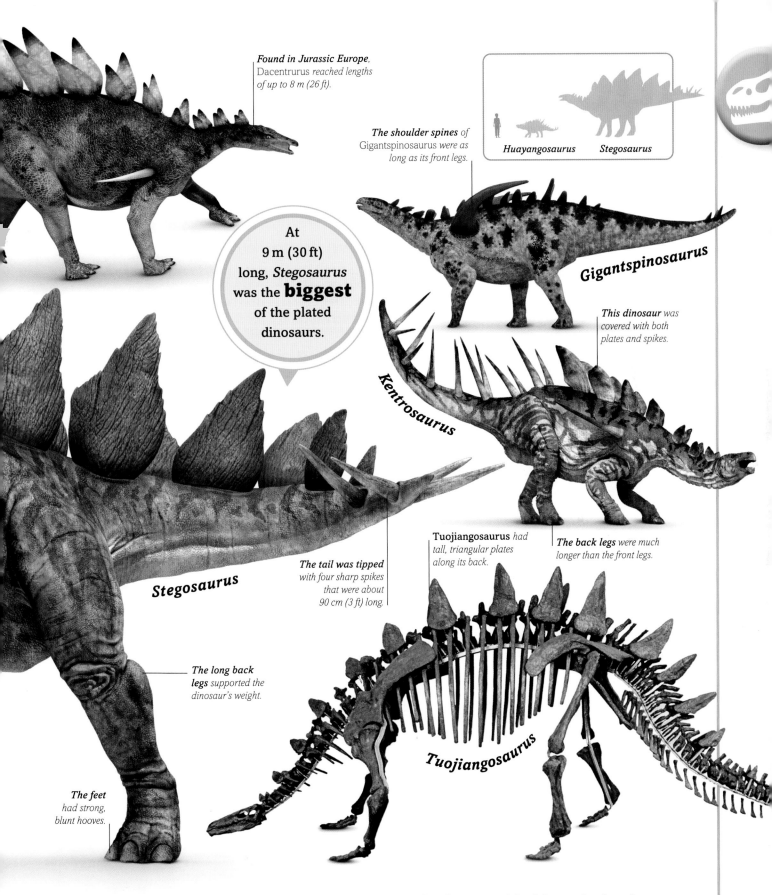

Found in Jurassic Europe, Dacentrurus *reached lengths of up to 8 m (26 ft).*

The shoulder spines of Gigantspinosaurus *were as long as its front legs.*

Huayangosaurus   Stegosaurus

At 9 m (30 ft) long, *Stegosaurus* was the **biggest** of the plated dinosaurs.

Gigantspinosaurus

This dinosaur *was covered with both plates and spikes.*

Kentrosaurus

Tuojiangosaurus *had tall, triangular plates along its back.*

The back legs *were much longer than the front legs.*

The tail was tipped *with four sharp spikes that were about 90 cm (3 ft) long.*

Stegosaurus

The long back legs *supported the dinosaur's weight.*

The feet *had strong, blunt hooves.*

Tuojiangosaurus

used for defence, while the spikes on the end of a stegosaur's tail would certainly have been used to lash out at a predator. But the spectacular plates may have been brightly coloured to attract a mate. All stegosaurs were plant-eaters, with narrow, beaked mouths that were ideal for gathering the most nourishing parts of low-growing shrubs and other plants. They also had the smallest brain of any dinosaur – the elephant-sized *Stegosaurus* had a brain that was no bigger than a dog's.

About tails

The vicious spikes at the tip of the tail could easily kill an attacking hunter.

Caudipteryx *had a short, stiffened tail with a distinctive fan of feathers.*

Caudipteryx

Huayangosaurus

The weight of its tail helped Spinosaurus keep its balance on land and in water.

Spinosaurus

The biggest dinosaur yet found had a slender, mobile tail tip for flicking enemies aside.

Although built like a bird, Caudipteryx had short front limbs and could not fly.

Patagotitan

Traces of colour cells in the fossils of this small hunter show that its tail had a pattern of light and dark bands.

Lesothosaurus

Sinosauropteryx

Big muscles *attached to the base of the tail helped power the dinosaur's legs.*

The sharp spikes on the tail made it an effective weapon for defence.

Shunosaurus

Whether long, spiked, clubbed, or feathered, dinosaur tails had different uses. Most of the big dinosaurs had long, bony tails equipped with powerful muscles. These heavy tails helped to balance the weight of the dinosaur's head and upper body. This was especially important for dinosaurs like **Xiongguanlong** that walked on their hind legs. The giant sauropod **Patagotitan** however, could sweep its long tail sideways like a whip with enough speed and force to knock a predator off its

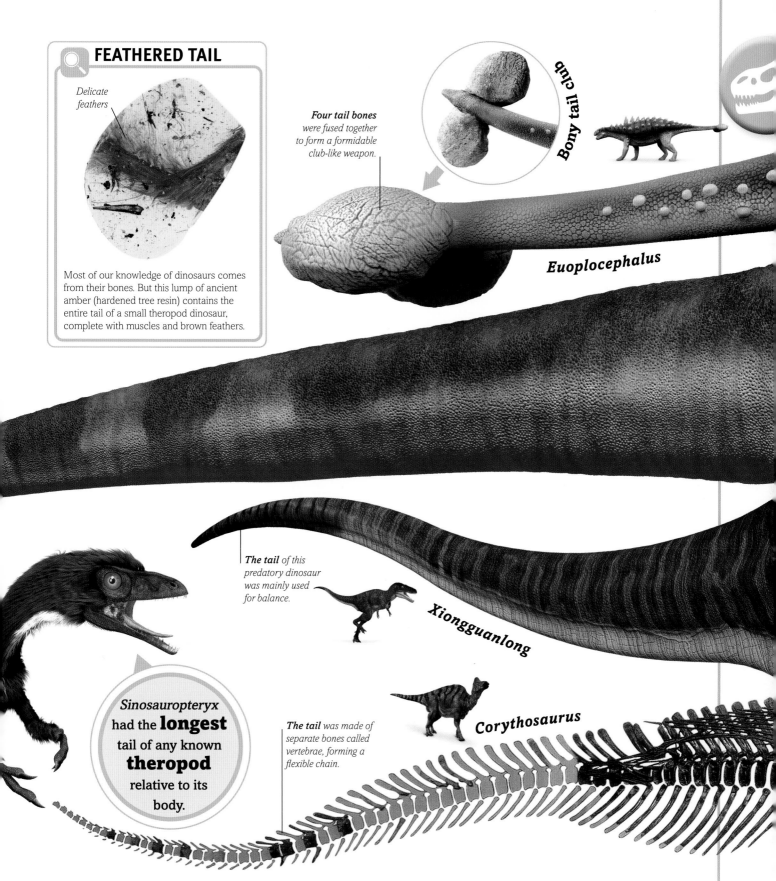

FEATHERED TAIL

Delicate feathers

Most of our knowledge of dinosaurs comes from their bones. But this lump of ancient amber (hardened tree resin) contains the entire tail of a small theropod dinosaur, complete with muscles and brown feathers.

Four tail bones were fused together to form a formidable club-like weapon.

Bony tail club

Euoplocephalus

The tail of this predatory dinosaur was mainly used for balance.

Xiongguanlong

Sinosauropteryx had the **longest** tail of any known **theropod** relative to its body.

The tail was made of separate bones called vertebrae, forming a flexible chain.

Corythosaurus

feet. The tail of **Huayangosaurus** was armed with two pairs of sharp spikes at the tip that made it a formidable weapon; the mid-sized sauropod **Shunosaurus** had a similar adaptation. Some ankylosaurs like **Euoplocephalus** had a massive, bony tail club that could be slammed into an enemy like a sledgehammer, shattering its bones. Some small theropod dinosaurs like **Caudipteryx** had short, bony tails with long feathers, just like modern birds. They may have been used for balance or to attract a mate.

77

DEADLY SPIKES

For a hungry predator like *Ceratosaurus*, which lived in North America and Europe about 155 million years ago, a big, slow-moving stegosaur like *Dacentrurus* would have made a tempting target. The tall spikes on the stegosaur's back and tail certainly looked imposing, but could they cause any harm? Moving in to launch its attack, *Ceratosaurus* would soon find out – the hard way.

A hole in the tail bone belonging to another Jurassic predator, *Allosaurus,* was found to be a perfect match with a *Stegosaurus* tail spike. It is likely that the stegosaur was defending itself from an attack by swinging its tail like a spiked club. *Dacentrurus* was equipped in exactly the same way, with two pairs of stout, sharp-pointed spikes at the end of its tail. If an enemy like *Ceratosaurus* tried to creep up from behind – a common predatory tactic – it would be in for a nasty shock. With a flick of its spiked tail, the stegosaur could inflict terrible damage, blinding or even killing the hunter outright. It might have been a slow-moving plant-eater, but *Dacentrurus* could look after itself.

Ankylosaurs

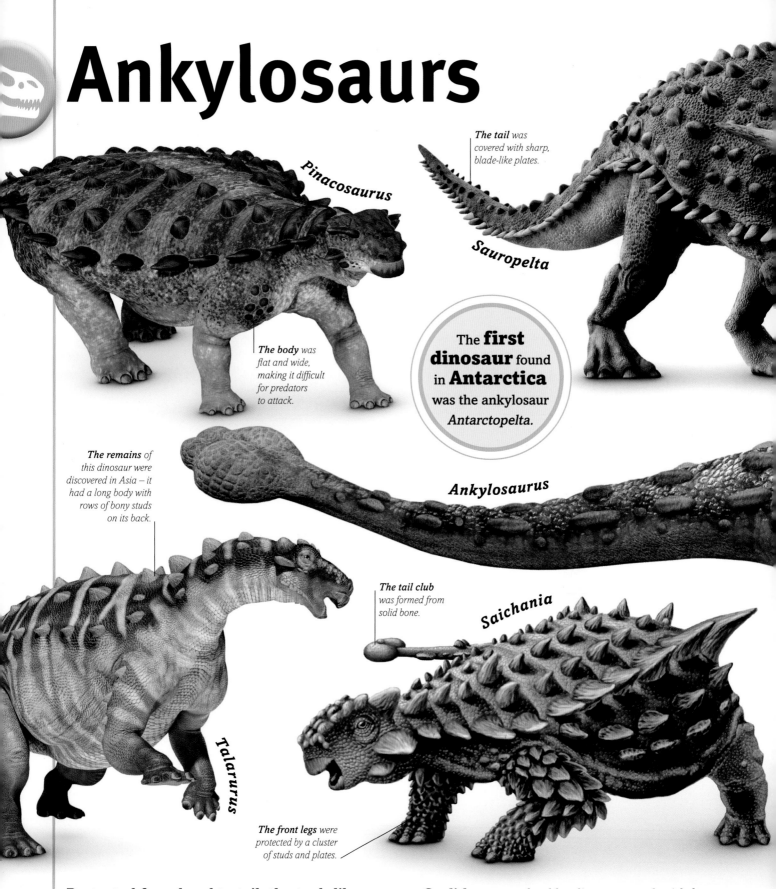

Pinacosaurus

The tail was covered with sharp, blade-like plates.

Sauropelta

The body was flat and wide, making it difficult for predators to attack.

The **first dinosaur** found in **Antarctica** was the ankylosaur Antarctopelta.

The remains of this dinosaur were discovered in Asia – it had a long body with rows of bony studs on its back.

Ankylosaurus

The tail club was formed from solid bone.

Saichania

Talarurus

The front legs were protected by a cluster of studs and plates.

Protected from head to tail, the tank-like ankylosaurs first appeared about 170 million years ago. They were slow-moving plant-eaters, so without their body armour they would have been easy targets for predators. Early ankylosaur relatives such as *Scelidosaurus* had bodies covered with bony plates and studs strong enough to break the teeth of any attacking dinosaur. But as predators got bigger and more powerful, ankylosaurs such as *Saichania* developed thick armour that may have discouraged even the massive-jawed

Hungarosaurus

| Hungarosaurus | Ankylosaurus |

Rows of spikes jutted from the sides of Hungarosaurus.

Gargoyleosaurus

Armour plates protected the heads of some ankylosaurs.

Sauropelta had long spikes on its neck.

The bony plates were embedded in the thick skin.

Ankylosaurus *even had armoured eyelids.*

Like many ankylosaurs, only the belly was unprotected.

Scelidosaurus

The beak of this ankylosaur ancestor had sharp edges for cropping plants.

tyrannosaurs. Like several others, including **Ankylosaurus**, *Saichania* also had a hefty tail club to swipe at predators, inflicting serious injury. Others, such as **Sauropelta**, had long shoulder spikes that may have been as much for show as for defence. Many had broad mouths, ideal for gathering plant food in bulk, without being too selective, much like modern elephants. Their bulky bodies contained big digestive systems for processing their fibrous diet.

Dinosaur defence

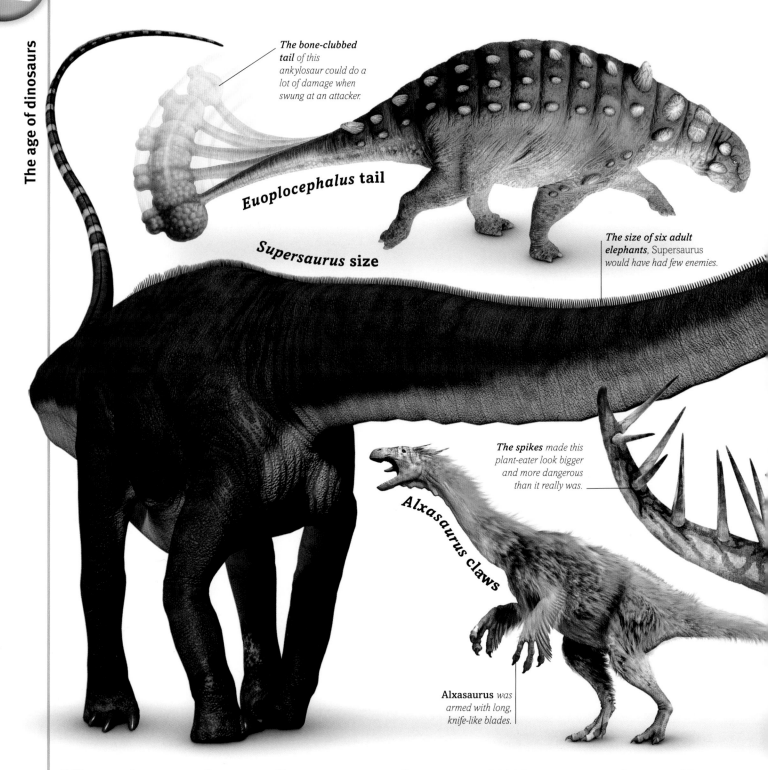

The bone-clubbed tail of this ankylosaur could do a lot of damage when swung at an attacker.

Euoplocephalus tail

Supersaurus size

The size of six adult elephants, Supersaurus would have had few enemies.

The spikes made this plant-eater look bigger and more dangerous than it really was.

Alxasaurus claws

Alxasaurus was armed with long, knife-like blades.

Life was dangerous for many dinosaurs. They faced powerful predators – fierce meat-eating theropods with huge jaws and big appetites. For a few giant dinosaurs like **Supersaurus**, their sheer size was enough to make hunters choose easier targets. Small dinosaurs could hide or run away from trouble as was the case with the ostrich-like dinosaur **Struthiomimus**. The stiff bristles on the back of **Heterodontosaurus** may have deterred enemies like the quills of porcupines. The big plant-eater **Kentrosaurus** ("spiked lizard") was

This small dinosaur's **back** was covered with prickly bristles.

Heterodontosaurus bristles

Some of the frill spikes were about 60 cm (24 in) long.

The **nose horn** of *Styracosaurus* may have been up to 57 cm (22 in) long.

Struthiomimus speed

With its long legs, Struthiomimus could outrun most of its enemies.

The reinforced skull of a pachycephalosaur could be used as a weapon in a crisis.

Styracosaurus horns

Pachycephalosaurus head

Kentrosaurus spikes

The extra-long shoulder spikes protected it from side attacks.

heavily armoured with plates and spikes. It could use its spiked tail as a defensive weapon, just like the club-tailed **Euoplocephalus**, lashing out at an attacker. **Styracosaurus** had an impressive array of horns, which may have been useful in a tight corner. Others like **Alxasaurus** had long, curved claws on its hands that could inflict serious damage, and the bone-headed **Pachycephalosaurus** may have even charged its enemies head first. Sometimes attack was the best form of defence.

Iguanodontians

Ouranosaurus

Ouranosaurus had a distinctive fin-like sail extending down the spine.

Dryosaurus

The sheep-sized Dryosaurus *had long feet and slender, powerful back legs, suggesting it was a fast runner.*

The sharp-edged beak was used for gathering plant food.

Tenontosaurus

Camptosaurus

The three long, sharp claws *on its hands would have enabled* Tenontosaurus *to swipe at a predator.*

The hand had a sharp thumb spike *that may have been used to stab attackers or for ripping tough plants.*

Among the very first dinosaur fossils to be discovered and scientifically identified was the tooth of an *Iguanodon* – one of the biggest plant-eating ornithopods. It was found in England in 1822, and given the name "iguana tooth" because of its similarity to the much smaller leaf-shaped teeth of present-day iguana lizards. Later, many entire skeletons of *Iguanodon* were found, with at least 38 discovered at one site in France, so it was probably a very common animal 135–125 million years ago. But *Iguanodon* was one of

Bulky body had plenty of space for a large stomach to process fibrous food.

Muttaburrasaurus

Fossils of this big dinosaur were found at Muttaburra in Australia.

Many of these dinosaurs may have had comb-like dorsal crests.

Rhabdodon

Iguanodon

The long, heavy tail helped balance its large body.

The back legs were longer and more powerful than the front legs, which helped support some of its weight.

The skull was narrow.

Mantellisaurus

Mantellisaurus had a short thumb spike.

The back legs were twice as long as the front limbs.

Rhabdodon   Iguanodon

many similar dinosaurs. They all had strong hind legs and shorter, weaker arms, and the smaller ones such as **Dryosaurus** may have walked on their hind legs. Many, including **Tenontosaurus**, **Muttaburrasaurus**, and the elephant-sized *Iguanodon* itself, were more heavily built and supported some of their weight with their forelimbs. Despite this, their hands were adapted for a variety of tasks, with hoof-like middle fingers, a mobile grasping fifth finger, and a stout spike on the thumb that may have been used as a defensive weapon.

Plant-eaters

Protoceratops

All ceratopsians *had closely packed cheek teeth for chopping up leaves.*

Diplodocus

Nigersaurus

Diplodocus *used its peg-like teeth like a rake.*

This **dinosaur** had more than **1,000** teeth.

Edmontosaurus

Hadrosaur

The front of the jaw supported a broad beak.

Plant-eating dinosaurs used their teeth in different ways. The long-necked sauropods and their relatives – animals like **Diplodocus** – had specialized front teeth for gathering plants. Some used their teeth like combs to strip leaves from the twigs of trees and bushes. Many do not seem to have chewed their food, and just swallowed the leaves whole. Other plant-eaters like **Edmontosaurus** and **Psittacosaurus** had sharp beaks for gathering food, and specially adapted cheek teeth for chewing it. The teeth of some of these animals, such as **Iguanodon**,

Camarasaurus's long, peg-like teeth were for raking through foliage.

Camarasaurus

JAW MOVEMENT

Most modern plant-eating animals chew their food. This involves grinding their teeth together using complex jaw movements – up and down, side to side, or forwards and backwards. The skulls and jaw bones of plant-eating dinosaurs show that some of these animals did the same. The jaws of *Psittacosaurus* and many hadrosaurs could slide forwards and backwards, and ankylosaurs could probably chew by moving their jaws from side to side, just like sheep.

Jaw closing muscles were attached to rigid cheekbones.

Jaw joint

Jaws could slide forwards and backwards.

Psittacosaurus

Iguanodon

Iguanodon's flattened teeth had serrated edges.

The leaf-shaped teeth were ideal for snipping leaves from the twigs.

Jobaria

The front teeth were specialized for cropping low-growing plants.

The parrot-like beak was used to gather plant food and may even have been used to crack nuts.

Psittacosaurus

Hundreds of teeth formed a complex grinding surface.

were saw-edged for cutting up leaves, but hadrosaurs such as *Edmontosaurus* had hundreds of teeth packed together to form a file-like surface, specialized for reducing leaves and other plant material to a pulp. This made food much easier to digest, so the hadrosaurs did not need to spend so much of their time eating. As with all dinosaurs, the old, damaged teeth were continuously replaced by new ones, so they never wore out.

Hadrosaurs

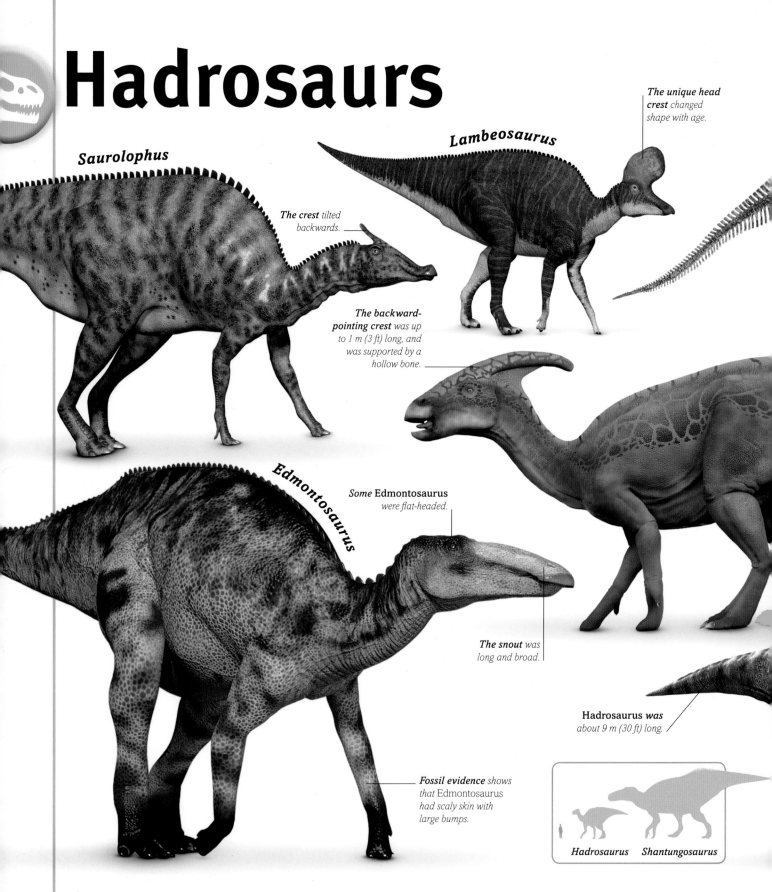

Saurolophus

Lambeosaurus

The unique head crest changed shape with age.

The crest tilted backwards.

The backward-pointing crest was up to 1 m (3 ft) long, and was supported by a hollow bone.

Edmontosaurus

Some Edmontosaurus were flat-headed.

The snout was long and broad.

Hadrosaurus was about 9 m (30 ft) long.

Fossil evidence shows that Edmontosaurus had scaly skin with large bumps.

Hadrosaurus   *Shantungosaurus*

Hadrosaurs lived during the Cretaceous Period, between 100–66 million years ago. They roamed the forests and swamps of North and South America, Europe, and Asia. They were large plant-eaters, and many of them had a broad, duck-like beak that they used to crop leaves. Similar to earlier iguanodontians, but with more complex teeth and jaws, hadrosaurs had jaws lined with hundreds of teeth arranged like the teeth of a file. Grinding together, these teeth reduced tough plant food to a juicy, easily digested pulp, ensuring that a

Maiasaura

The helmet-like crest was brightly coloured to impress potential mates.

The back had a high, bony ridge.

Corythosaurus

The fossils of young **Maiasaura** *show that like all young animals, it had a large head, eyes, and feet until the rest of the body caught up.*

About 15 m (49 ft) in length, Shantungosaurus *is the largest known hadrosaur.*

Parasaurolophus

Shantungosaurus

The jaw was studded with more than 1,500 chewing teeth.

Hadrosaurus

Hadrosaurus was the **first dinosaur** to be unearthed in North America.

The small front feet did not bear much weight.

hadrosaur, such as **Edmontosaurus**, got as much nutrition as possible from every mouthful. Many hadrosaurs, including **Lambeosaurus**, also had impressive crests on their heads that could have been used to attract mates or for temperature control. The crests of some, such as **Parasaurolophus**, formed bony tubes that may have helped to amplify their calls, making them sound like trumpeting elephants. They lived in herds, calling to each other to stay in contact as they roamed the forests of the Cretaceous world.

Cool crests

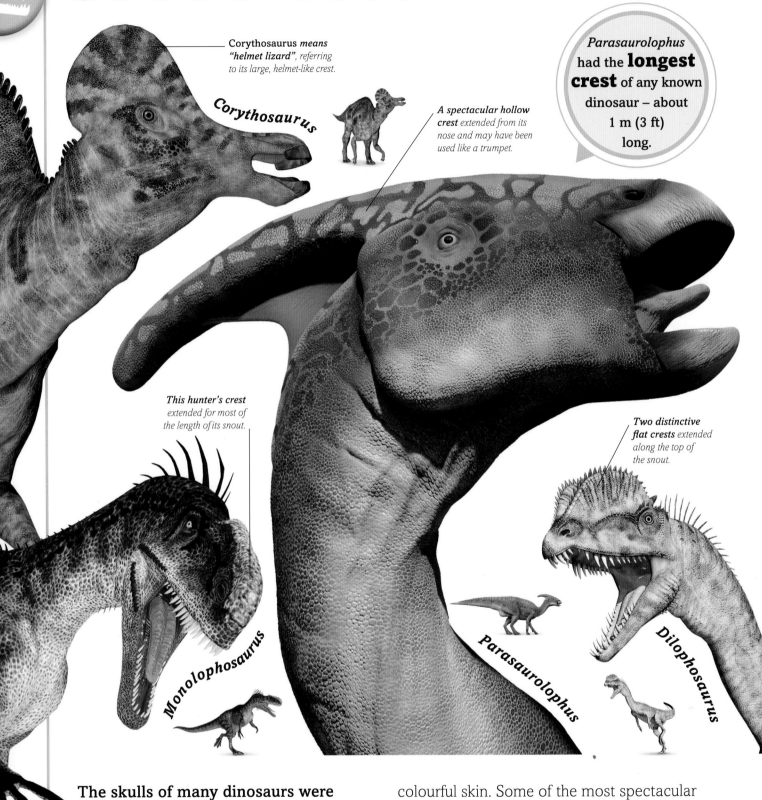

Corythosaurus *means "helmet lizard", referring to its large, helmet-like crest.*

Corythosaurus

A spectacular hollow crest extended from its nose and may have been used like a trumpet.

Parasaurolophus had the **longest crest** of any known dinosaur – about 1 m (3 ft) long.

This hunter's crest extended for most of the length of its snout.

Two distinctive flat crests extended along the top of the snout.

Monolophosaurus

Parasaurolophus

Dilophosaurus

The skulls of many dinosaurs were equipped with bony features that may have supported impressive crests. The bones were probably extended by extra structures made of tough keratin, like the horns of cattle or sheep, or covered by colourful skin. Some of the most spectacular crests belonged to hadrosaurs, such as **Corythosaurus**, **Olorotitan**, and especially **Parasaurolophus**. The bones of these crests were hollow – possibly to make their calls louder, since the chambers in the crests of

At the top of the
skull *was a thin sheet of
bone that curled forwards.*

Cryolophosaurus

The skin *covering the
fan-shaped crest was probably
patterned with bright colours.*

Olorotitan

Lambeosaurus

**The unusual
axe-shaped crest**
*curved forwards
over the skull.*

A bony ridge
*supported its crest
of tough keratin.*

Citipati

many hadrosaurs were linked to their nostrils. But hadrosaurs were not the only crested dinosaurs. Several predatory theropods had crests too, including the double-crested **Dilophosaurus** and a dinosaur found in Antarctica, **Cryolophosaurus**. Crests were also a prominent feature of beaked, bird-like oviraptorids like **Citipati**. All these bony extensions were for show, much like the colourful feathers of many modern-day birds.

Dinosaur eggs

This dinosaur egg *was about the size of a basketball.*

Sauropod egg

The nest was a **mound of earth** *lined with ferns and twigs.*

Maiasaura nest

Tiny at first, young dinosaurs grew very quickly.

Saltasaurus

Thousands of **Saltasaurus eggs** were found in one nesting site – they were laid 80 MYA.

Just like their closest living relatives, birds and crocodiles, all dinosaurs laid eggs. Some dinosaur eggs were leathery and soft-shelled, but most had hard, chalky shells like birds' eggs, and at some fossil sites, the ground is covered in shell fragments. Where the eggs are intact, they have clearly been laid in nests on the ground. The biggest dinosaurs such as the **sauropods** seem to have buried their eggs in warm earth, or in piles of warm, decaying vegetation like modern crocodiles. The warmth was essential to make them hatch. Many smaller, lighter dinosaurs like

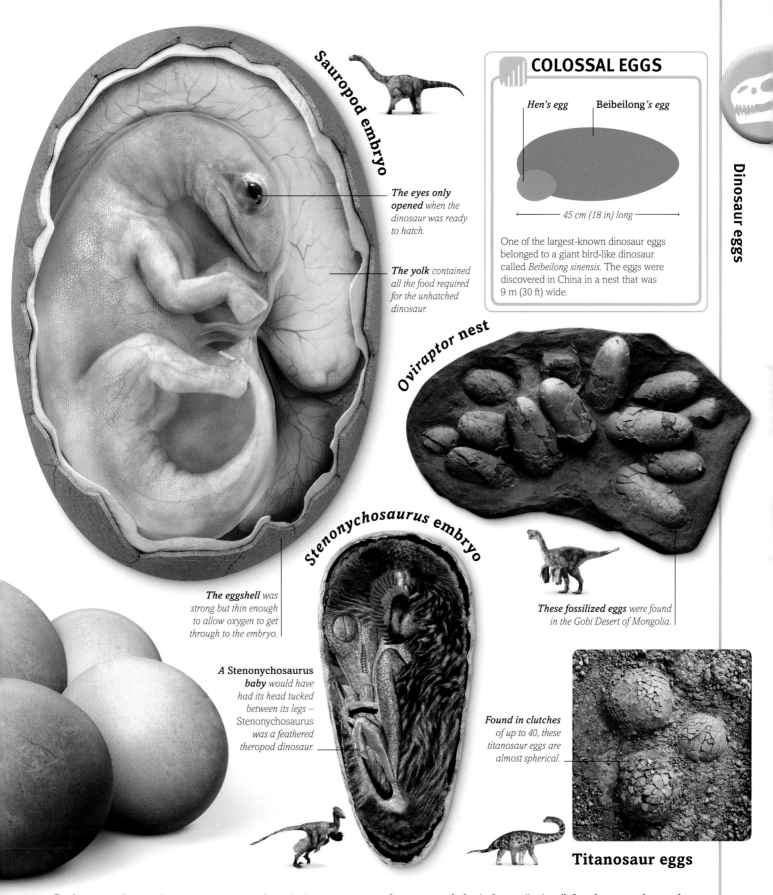

Sauropod embryo

The eyes only opened when the dinosaur was ready to hatch.

The yolk contained all the food required for the unhatched dinosaur.

COLOSSAL EGGS

Hen's egg   Beibeilong's egg

45 cm (18 in) long

One of the largest-known dinosaur eggs belonged to a giant bird-like dinosaur called *Beibeilong sinensis*. The eggs were discovered in China in a nest that was 9 m (30 ft) wide.

Oviraptor nest

Stenonychosaurus embryo

The eggshell was strong but thin enough to allow oxygen to get through to the embryo.

A Stenonychosaurus *baby* would have had its head tucked between its legs – Stenonychosaurus was a feathered theropod dinosaur.

These fossilized eggs were found in the Gobi Desert of Mongolia.

Found in clutches of up to 40, these titanosaur eggs are almost spherical.

Titanosaur eggs

Oviraptor kept their eggs warm by sitting on them, just as most modern birds do. We know this because the fossilized remains of the adult dinosaurs have been found sitting on their eggs. The long-armed, feathered theropod dinosaurs known as maniraptorans may even have used their long "wing" feathers to brood and protect their eggs. The adults of some dinosaurs such as the hadrosaur *Maiasaura* ("good mother lizard"), cared for their newly hatched young, bringing food for them and driving away predators.

93

DINOSAUR CRÈCHE
Around 125 million years ago a catastrophic mudflow or fall of volcanic ash, in what is now eastern China, overwhelmed a nest of baby *Psittacosaurus*. They were buried along with a half-grown adult, just six years old. Found in 2004, their fossils seem to prove that the babies were being cared for after hatching, and that their carer might not even be their parent.

Many modern animals, from songbirds to wolves, live in extended families where the half-grown young help their parents look after the babies. Some birds such as ostriches also lay their eggs in communal nests, or guard their young in crèches. The *Psittacosaurus* nest contained a huge family of 34 young. It seems likely that they had more than one mother, and that they were being looked after by a babysitter – probably the elder sister or brother of some of the babies. If so, such childcare may have been common among dinosaurs. *Psittacosaurus* was an early ceratopsian – an ancestor of animals like *Triceratops*. Maybe these horned giants looked after their young in the same way.

Pachycephalosaurs

Homalocephale   Pachycephalosaurus

Acrotholus

Numerous small spikes lined the head, snout, and cheeks.

The bony shelf was a distinctive feature of all pachycephalosaurs.

Stegoceras

Discovered in Canada in 2013, Acrotholus was about 1.8 m (6 ft) long.

The big eye sockets indicate that these dinosaurs had good vision.

The long horns may have been for display rather than fighting.

Stygimoloch

The sharp beak was used to gather leaves, fruit, and possibly insects.

Dracorex

Small hands were useful for collecting food.

Also known as "boneheads", referring to their incredibly thick, strong skulls, pachycephalosaurs were unusual looking dinosaurs. The largest of the boneheads was *Pachycephalosaurus*. Its skull alone, the biggest so far, was up to 40 cm (16 in) thick, and ringed with small, bony spikes. It is likely that the strong skull protected the animal's brain from regular impact inflicted during fights with rivals over status. But not all pachycephalosaurs had the same skull form. The smaller *Homalocephale* had a flat-topped head,

The flat-topped skull was not well adapted to withstand impact.

Homalocephale

Prenocephale had a rounded, sloping head.

Prenocephale

Pachycephalosaurus

The long and powerful hind legs supported the dinosaur's weight.

Only a **skull** of *Pachycephalosaurus* has been **discovered**.

THICK-SKULLED

The top of the skull was solid bone.

The skull of *Pachycephalosaurus* was 20 times thicker than other dinosaur skulls and cushioned a relatively small brain. The bone often has evidence of damage, supporting the theory that they may have used their skulls for head-butting combats.

and **Stygimoloch** had a small dome with much longer horns. But some scientists think these smaller animals are just younger specimens of *Pachycephalosaurus*. Even though the fossil remains of these dinosaurs are very rare, enough have been found to show that pachycephalosaurs were probably fast, agile animals. The fossils also show that they had leaf-shaped teeth like other plant-eating dinosaurs, and sharp pointed teeth at the front of their jaws, suggesting that they may have eaten a variety of plant and animal food.

Ceratopsians

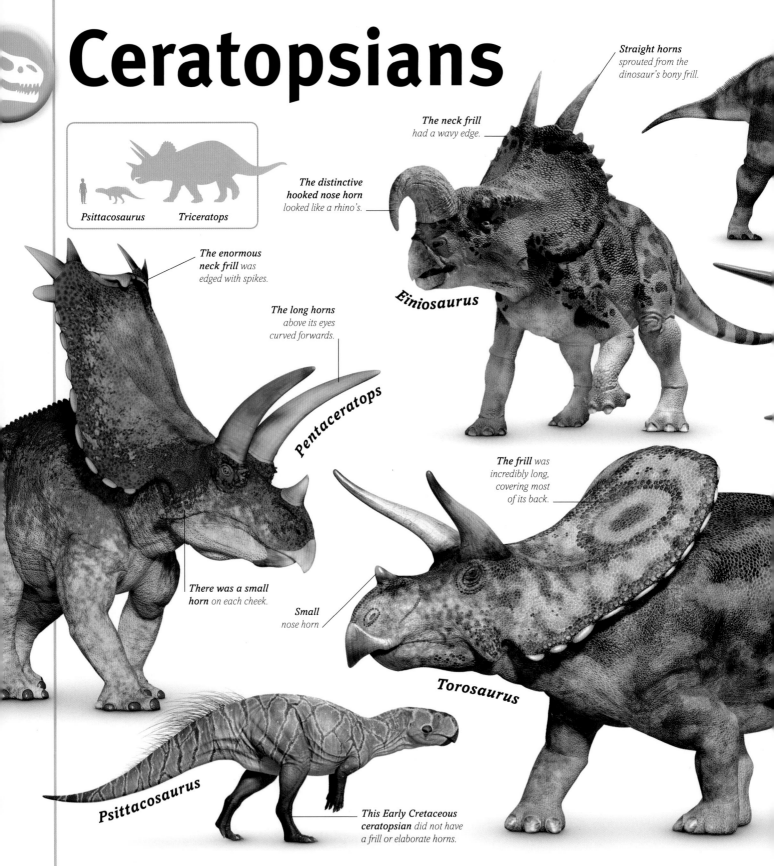

Psittacosaurus Triceratops

Straight horns *sprouted from the dinosaur's bony frill.*

The neck frill *had a wavy edge.*

The distinctive hooked nose horn *looked like a rhino's.*

Einiosaurus

The enormous neck frill *was edged with spikes.*

The long horns *above its eyes curved forwards.*

Pentaceratops

The frill *was incredibly long, covering most of its back.*

There was a small horn *on each cheek.*

Small *nose horn*

Torosaurus

Psittacosaurus

This Early Cretaceous ceratopsian *did not have a frill or elaborate horns.*

With their elaborate neck frills, huge horns, and parrot-like beaks, the ceratopsians were among the most spectacular dinosaurs. The most well-known, **Triceratops**, was an elephant-sized animal with three horns up to 1.5 m (5 ft) long and a big bony frill extending from the back of its skull. **Pentaceratops** was even more flamboyant, with an enormous, probably brightly coloured frill fringed by spikes. It evolved from smaller ancestors such as **Psittacosaurus**, which was light enough to walk on two legs, but the later giants needed all four

The neck frill was circular.

Nasutoceratops *had unusual forward-facing horns.*

Nasutoceratops

The frill was mostly coloured skin supported by a bony frame.

Chasmosaurus

These long horns had sharp tips.

Triceratops

The upright, **curved horns** *gave* Diabloceratops *a devilish appearance.*

The massive *parrot-like beak helped it to rip off tough vegetation.*

Diabloceratops

Sturdy weight-bearing feet had stout hooves on each toe.

feet to support their weight. The ceratopsians were plant-eaters, equipped with a grasping beak and closely packed teeth that cut through tough leaves like scissors. As with all dinosaurs, the worn-out teeth were continuously replaced by new ones, so their shearing jaws never became blunt. Ceratopsians lived in herds as a possible defence strategy against predators. Fossil evidence suggests they were common in western North America about 74–66 million years ago. *Triceratops* itself was one of the last giant dinosaurs to roam the Earth.

HEAD TO HEAD
Armed with its enormous nose horn and magnificent spiky frill, *Styracosaurus* would have been an impressive sight. The size and weight of a rhinoceros, it roamed the forests of North America about 75–74 million years ago, feeding on low-growing plants. Its large frill covered the back of its neck while six long spikes flared out from the frill.

Styracosaurus lived in the same region and time as the tyrannosaurs *Gorgosaurus* and *Daspletosaurus* – both formidable predators that would have seen it as potential prey. If attacked, *Styracosaurus* may have defended itself with its stout, sharp nose horn. But the dramatic crown around its frill would have had little defensive value, and it probably evolved to impress other dinosaurs of its own species. Males may have competed for territory and mates just like modern bison and deer, and the male with the most imposing array of horns would have had few challengers. But if two rivals were closely matched, they may have fought in head to head combat until one backed off in defeat.

Herds and packs

Corythosaurus *may have used air passages* in its crest *to make booming calls.*

Corythosaurus alarm call

Lythronax pack hunting

Attacked from behind, the horned Centrosaurus *didn't stand a chance of escaping.*

A bone bed of **thousands** of *Centrosaurus* fossils show they may have lived in a herd.

Dinosaurs did not live alone. We know from their fossilized footprints that many travelled in big groups, especially giant sauropods and other plant-eaters. Living in a herd had many advantages for herbivores like **Corythosaurus**; some animals could concentrate on eating while others kept watch and sounded the alarm if danger threatened. Vulnerable animals could also be protected by several adults, and a dinosaur in a herd was less likely to be targeted than an animal on its own. Some meat-eaters may also have

Travelling together *in search of food made long journeys less risky.*

Europasaurus herd migrating

By combining strength, *small hunters could bring down larger prey.*

Deinonychus pack hunting

Chasmosaurus may have defended their young by forming a protective circle, turning their horns towards the predator.

Daspletosaurus

Chasmosaurus defence

lived in groups. While big tyrannosaurs such as **Daspletosaurus** probably hunted alone, smaller ones like **Lythronax** may have joined forces to bring down larger prey. Several skeletons of the wolf-sized **Deinonychus** have been found near the remains of the big, plant-eating *Tenontosaurus,* suggesting that they attacked it in a pack. They were almost certainly not smart enough to devise joint tactics. But they may have learned from experience that they were more likely to get a meal if they all targeted the same victim.

Early theropods

Liliensternus

Although Liliensternus *had the same slender, agile build as* Coelophysis, *it was twice as long and much more powerful.*

Big muscles *linking the dinosaur's legs to the base of its heavy tail added to its power and speed.*

The flared, bony crest *may have been brightly coloured to make the dinosaur look more impressive to mates and rivals.*

Cryolophosaurus

Cryolophosaurus was the **first theropod** to be discovered in Antarctica.

Massive thigh muscles *made the hind legs very strong, giving* Cryolophosaurus *the speed it needed to catch its prey.*

Coelophysis

The slender head *and flexible neck were adapted for seizing small, fast-moving animals.*

Theropods ran on three toes, *leaving distinctive three-toed footprints that are often found fossilized in rocks.*

The most powerful, terrifying dinosaurs were those that hunted other dinosaurs. These predators were theropods – animals that ran on two legs, balancing their bodies and typically heavy, strong-jawed skulls with the help of their long tails. They were very successful, evolving into many different types throughout the Mesozoic Era (also known as the age of dinosaurs) and are still thriving today in the form of birds. The first theropods evolved in the Late Triassic Period, about 230 million years ago, and were small, lightly built animals. They soon

Gasosaurus

Gojirasaurus

Dubreuillosaurus

Monolophosaurus

The jaws were full of curved, serrated, blade-like teeth that could slice through scaly skin and meat.

All theropods walked on their powerful hind legs, leaving their arms free for catching prey.

The unusually long skull was studded with sharp, pointed teeth.

Typical theropods had three-fingered hands, armed with strong claws for gripping prey.

Monolophosaurus had a distinctive bumpy crest.

Coelophysis   Gojirasaurus

evolved into slender, agile hunters like **Coelophysis**, one of the most successful early theropods, and its close relative, the bigger **Liliensternus**. Meanwhile, much more powerful hunters were evolving, and by the Early to Middle Jurassic Period, 200–165 million years ago, there were many big, powerful theropods, including **Cryolophosaurus** and the horse-sized **Dubreuillosaurus**. This period also saw the evolution of the first giant hunters, but the famous, far more lethal tyrannosaurs did not appear until much later.

Spinosaurids

Baryonyx

The sail *ran the length of its back and was supported by rod-like bones measuring up to 1.8 m (6 ft).*

The best fossils of *Spinosaurus* were **destroyed** by a wartime bombing raid in 1944.

Baryonyx *had a huge, heavy thumb claw for catching fish.*

Spinosaurus

The long, narrow snout *had conical teeth that were perfect for seizing slippery fish.*

This dinosaur had a wavy sail *that dipped at the hip.*

Ichthyovenator

Instead of a sail, **Suchomimus** *had a low ridge running down its back.*

Suchomimus

Irritator **had a bony crest** *that extended over its eyes.*

Big, sharp, curved claws *gave Suchomimus a good grip on its victims.*

Irritator

Irritator   Spinosaurus

The biggest predatory dinosaur ever found is the spectacular *Spinosaurus.* At up to 14 m (46 ft) long, this large dinosaur was one of a small group of similar hunters with jaws and teeth that were just like those of a modern crocodile. It is likely that they used them in the same way – to catch big fish in shallow water. But we know that they also ate other dinosaurs, because a fossil of **Baryonyx** has been found with the remains of a young *Iguanodon* in its stomach.

Allosauroids

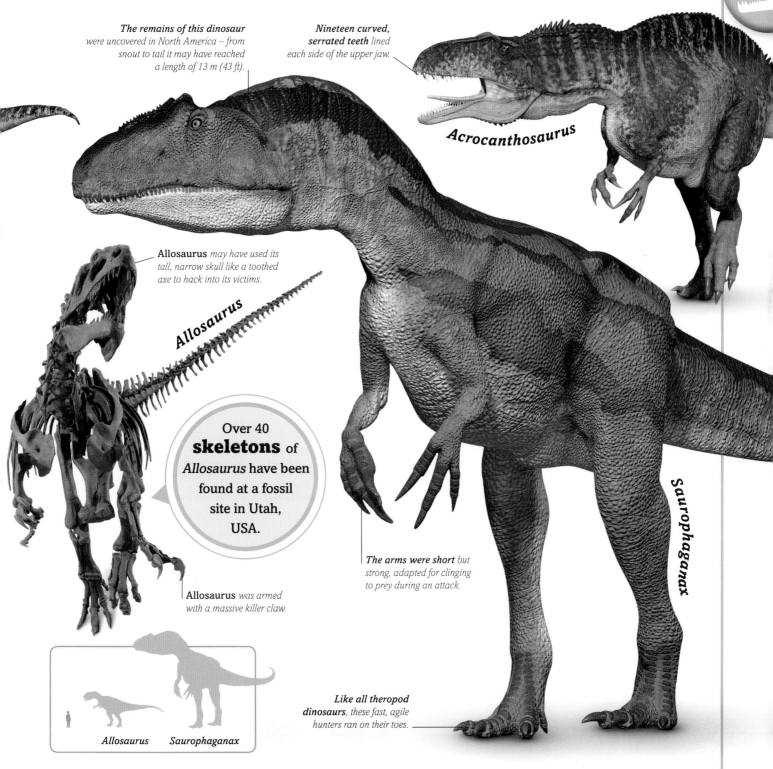

The remains of this dinosaur were uncovered in North America – from snout to tail it may have reached a length of 13 m (43 ft).

Nineteen curved, serrated teeth lined each side of the upper jaw.

Acrocanthosaurus

Allosaurus may have used its tall, narrow skull like a toothed axe to hack into its victims.

Allosaurus

Over 40 **skeletons** of *Allosaurus* have been found at a fossil site in Utah, USA.

Allosaurus was armed with a massive killer claw.

The arms were short but strong, adapted for clinging to prey during an attack.

Saurophaganax

Like all theropod dinosaurs, these fast, agile hunters ran on their toes.

Allosaurus   Saurophaganax

The main enemies of plant-eating dinosaurs during the Jurassic Period were fearsome hunters like *Allosaurus.*
This 8.5 m (28 ft) giant had a mouthful of teeth like steak knives, ideal for slicing through flesh. Over time, even bigger predators with the same type of weaponry evolved, including the colossal ***Saurophaganax***. This heavyweight hunter would have been able to overpower gigantic sauropods like the 23 m (75 ft) long *Apatosaurus*, whose fossils have been found in the same North American rocks.

Cutting edge

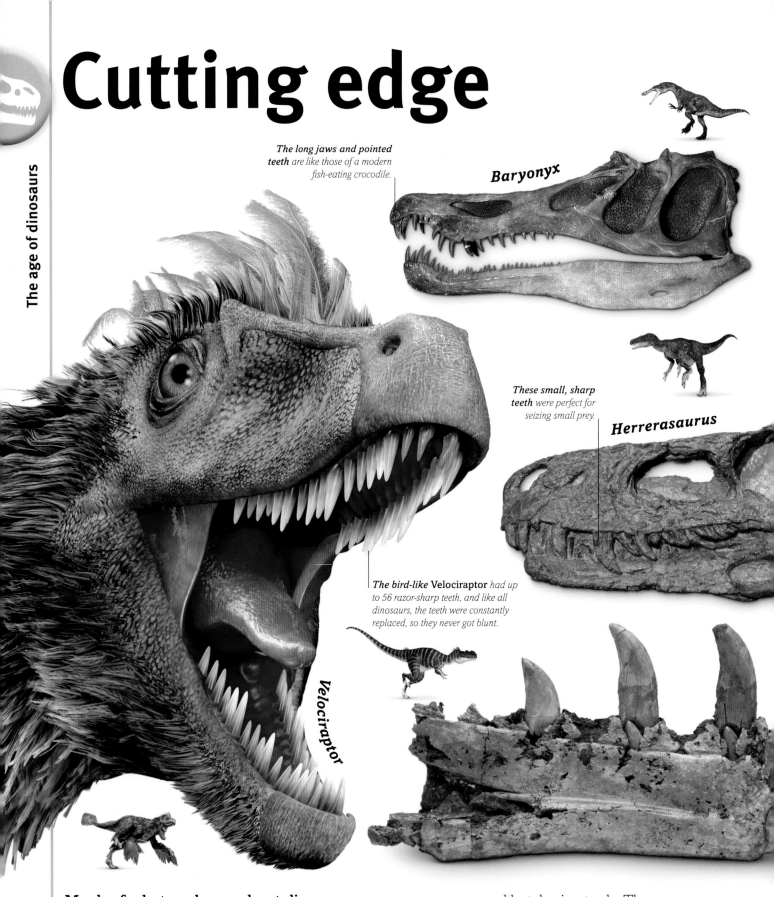

*The long jaws and pointed **teeth** are like those of a modern fish-eating crocodile.*

Baryonyx

*These small, sharp **teeth** were perfect for seizing small prey.*

Herrerasaurus

*The bird-like **Velociraptor** had up to 56 razor-sharp teeth, and like all dinosaurs, the teeth were constantly replaced, so they never got blunt.*

Velociraptor

Much of what we know about dinosaurs comes from their teeth. These were constantly replaced, so they never got blunt, and came in all shapes and sizes. The teeth of typical theropods like **Duriavenator** clearly belong to a carnivore, or meat-eater, used both as weapons and butchering tools. They were sharp, serrated blades, ideal for inflicting slashing wounds on prey and slicing the meat from their bones. They were useless for chewing, but since meat is easy to digest, mouthfuls could be swallowed without being chewed first.

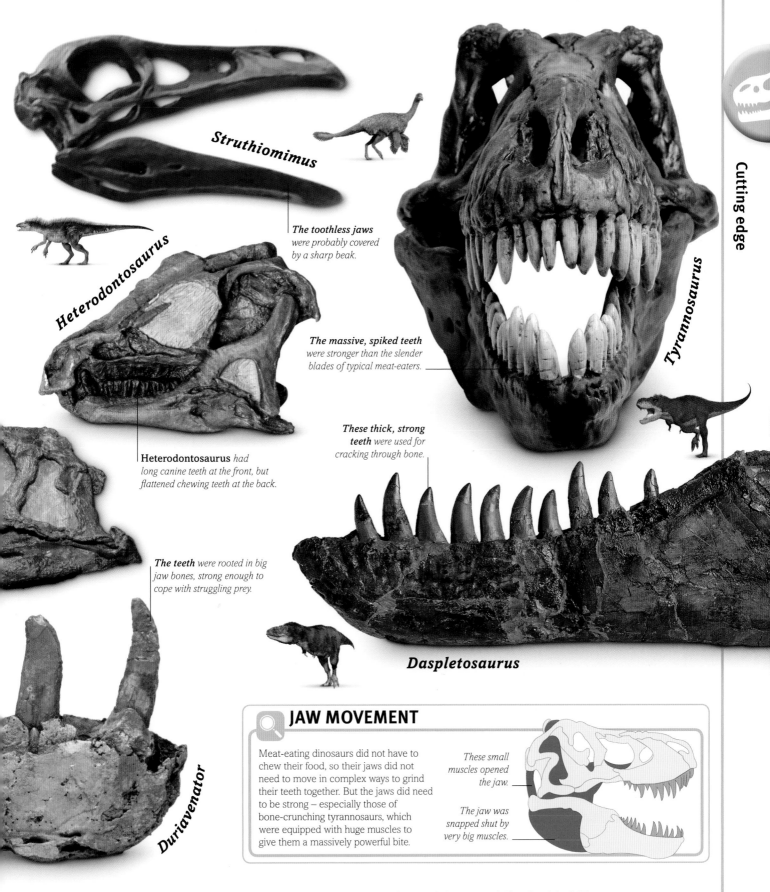

Struthiomimus

Heterodontosaurus

The toothless jaws were probably covered by a sharp beak.

The massive, spiked teeth were stronger than the slender blades of typical meat-eaters.

Tyrannosaurus

Heterodontosaurus *had long canine teeth at the front, but flattened chewing teeth at the back.*

These thick, strong teeth were used for cracking through bone.

The teeth were rooted in big jaw bones, strong enough to cope with struggling prey.

Daspletosaurus

Duriavenator

JAW MOVEMENT

Meat-eating dinosaurs did not have to chew their food, so their jaws did not need to move in complex ways to grind their teeth together. But the jaws did need to be strong – especially those of bone-crunching tyrannosaurs, which were equipped with huge muscles to give them a massively powerful bite.

These small muscles opened the jaw.

The jaw was snapped shut by very big muscles.

Different types of teeth suited different types of prey. **Velociraptor** had blade-like teeth ideal for attacking and eating other dinosaurs, but the pointed teeth in the jaws of **Baryonyx** were adapted for catching slippery fish. The massive spikes of **Tyrannosaurus** were perfect for biting through bone, while the bird-like **Struthiomimus** had no teeth at all. It may have eaten plants, small animals, or both. Unusually, **Heterodontosaurus** had several different types of teeth, which may have enabled it to eat both animals and plants.

109

Tyrannosaurs

Alioramus

Tarbosaurus

The jaw was very rigid, enabling it to hold on to struggling prey.

Daspletosaurus

Tarbosaurus *had the smallest arms of any tyrannosaur.*

The deep snout *helped to resist the stress created from biting through bone.*

Albertosaurus *had bony horns in front of its eyes.*

The heavy tail *balanced the weight of* Albertosaurus*'s massive head and jaws.*

Albertosaurus

The lightweight crest *was probably brightly coloured for display.*

The long legs *were built for speed, allowing* Albertosaurus *to charge into an attack.*

Guanlong

Guanlong   Tyrannosaurus

The tyrannosaurs ("tyrant lizards") were the most powerful land predators to walk the Earth. These theropods first appeared about 165 million years ago and thrived until the age of the dinosaurs came to an end 66 million years ago. The biggest of them all was *Tyrannosaurus* –

the ultimate heavyweight killer. Their weapons were their specialized teeth. Unlike other theropods, which had mouths full of sharp but fragile, knife-like teeth, the tyrannosaurs had stout spikes backed by powerful jaw muscles. This gave them the strength to bite straight

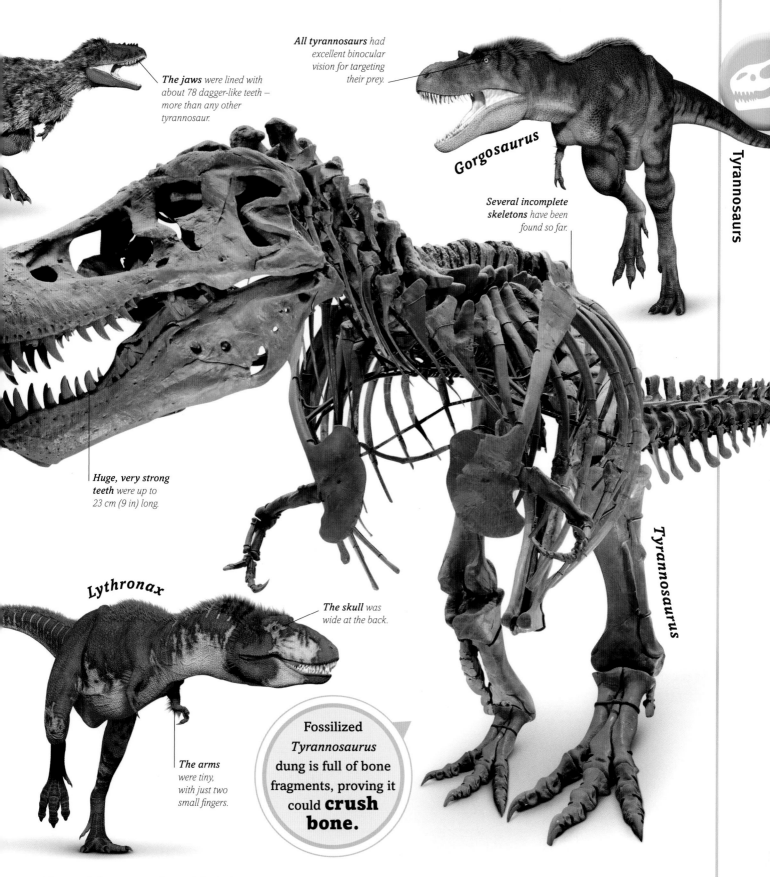

The jaws were lined with about 78 dagger-like teeth – more than any other tyrannosaur.

All tyrannosaurs had excellent binocular vision for targeting their prey.

Gorgosaurus

Several incomplete skeletons have been found so far.

Huge, very strong teeth were up to 23 cm (9 in) long.

Tyrannosaurus

Lythronax

The skull was wide at the back.

The arms were tiny, with just two small fingers.

Fossilized *Tyrannosaurus* dung is full of bone fragments, proving it could **crush bone.**

through bone, and enabled them to kill armoured prey that other predators dared not attack. Their jaws were so deadly that they did not need strong hands to grip their victims, and their arms were tiny compared to their long, muscular legs. Some of the earlier tyrannosaurs were more lightly built, including **Alioramus** and **Lythronax**, while others like **Guanlong** had crests on their heads. But all the ones that came later had a similar body structure – massive heads with a huge set of jaws mounted on a pair of powerful legs.

ULTIMATE HUNTER

Tyrannosaurus was one of the last of the giant dinosaurs, and one of the most lethal. Armed huge bone-crushing teeth and immense jaws that could inflict crippling bites, it was the top of its time. The strength of its bite was greater than that of almost any other predator in y, enabling it to subdue even elephant-sized animals such as this *Triceratops*.

Tyrannosaurus had a simple but effective technique when it came to attacking prey – it would charge straight in, sink its teeth into its target, and use its strong jaw and neck muscles to rip away mouthfuls of flesh and bone. Stunned by blood loss, the victim would not try to struggle free. So, *Tyrannosaurus* did not need to cling on to prevent its escape. Since strong forelimbs were not needed, they were reduced to tiny arms that couldn't even reach its mouth. By contrast, its legs were built like those of a racehorse, with massive thigh muscles and long, slender lower limbs. So, despite its immense weight, *Tyrannosaurus* would have launched its attacks with deadly speed.

Ornithomimosaurs

Found in China, Beishanlong *lived about 120 million years ago, and grew to about 8 m (26 ft) long.*

All these animals were covered in feathers, *but the feathers on the body probably had a simple hair-like structure.*

Beishanlong

The long snout *and deep lower jaw supported a broad beak similar to that of a duck.*

Gallimimus

For 50 years, the only known parts of *Deinocheirus* were its **huge arm bones**.

A long, slender, flexible neck *made it easy to pick up seeds and seize small animals.*

Struthiomimus

The legs had powerful muscles, *but were slim near the feet like the legs of all fast-running animals.*

The long feathers on the arms *may have been for display, or to protect eggs and young.*

Ornithomimus   Deinocheirus

The powerful, heavy-jawed tyrannosaurs had some close relatives that could hardly look less like them – the ornithomimosaurs. These included animals like **Struthiomimus**, which means "ostrich mimic", and they certainly resembled ostriches in many ways. Most ornithomimosaurs had small heads with toothless beaks, long necks, wing-like arms with fluffy feathers, and long, muscular back legs. They probably even had a similar diet of seeds, fruits, and small animals, although some had broader beaks that they may have used for dabbling in

Ornithomimus

The body *was built for speed and agility, just like a modern ostrich.*

The three-fingered hands *were unusually long.*

SPEEDSTERS

Long-legged ornithomimosaurs could run very fast. Recent studies show that their biggest enemies, tyrannosaurs, could run at 30 km/h (19 mph), so ornithomimosaurs probably ran faster – maybe as fast as Jamaican athlete Usain Bolt who reached 44 km/h (27 mph) in 2009.

Usain Bolt   Ornithomimus

Deinocheirus

The lightweight skull *supported a beak made of keratin, just like the beak of a modern bird.*

Anserimimus

The big, blunt claws *were probably used for defence.*

Big eyes *gave these animals the good vision they needed to watch out for danger.*

Qiupalong

The tail *may have ended in a fan of long feathers, which would have helped with balance while running.*

The feet *had specialized shock-absorbing bones for coping with the stresses of running.*

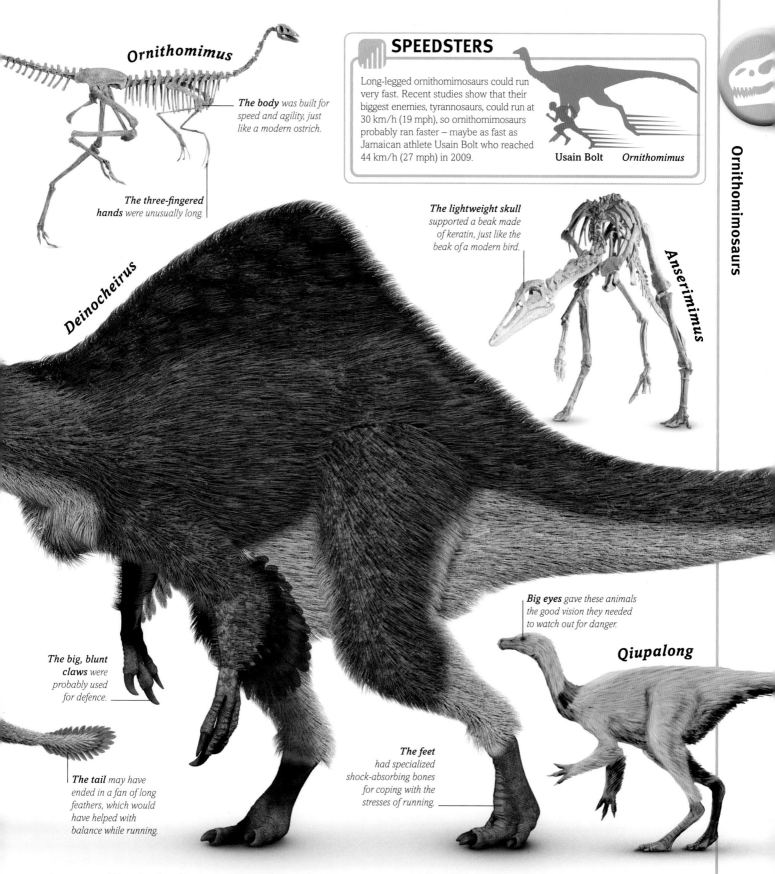

the water like ducks. But not all ornithomimosaurs were toothless or ostrich-sized. Some of the early types had jaws studded with small teeth, and some of the later ones like **Beishanlong** were big, powerful animals. The biggest found so far was **Deinocheirus**, a giant that grew to 11 m (36 ft) long and had very long arms and hands. Relative to its body, it had shorter legs than other ornithomimosaurs, so it probably relied on its size and big defensive claws to discourage the powerful predators of its time, and make them look for softer targets.

115

Oviraptorosaurs

Caudipteryx

The skull had **small teeth** at the front of the upper jaw, but no chewing teeth.

Long legs would have made Caudipteryx a fast runner.

Ajancingenia had a very short, deep skull with a powerful beak.

Ajancingenia

Anzu

The dinosaur could probably fan out the long feathers on its tail to enhance its displays.

About 8 m (26 ft) long and weighing as much as a car, this enormous oviraptorosaur is far bigger than any of its known relatives.

Huanansaurus

Discovered in 2015, **Huanansaurus** lived about 72 million years ago in what is now eastern China.

Like all oviraptorosaurs, **Gigantoraptor** almost certainly had long, flamboyant feathers on its arms.

In 1923 a group of American fossil hunters in Mongolia discovered the first complete dinosaur eggs. They also found the skull of an odd-looking dinosaur close by. They assumed it was trying to eat the eggs and called the dinosaur ***Oviraptor***, which means "egg thief".

Much later, in the 1990s, it became clear that the eggs were its own and that it was actually looking after them. Despite this, the name stuck, and is now used to describe several animals with the same features – the oviraptorosaurs. They belonged to a group

Discovered in North America, Anzu had a tall crest on its skull supported by a very thin sheet of bone.

Oviraptor

Caudipteryx **Gigantoraptor**

Oviraptor was **found** only 10 cm (4 in) away from the **egg nest.**

The lightly built **Oviraptor** *was about 1.8 m (6 ft) long.*

The end of each long finger *was equipped with a slender, gently curved claw.*

Chirostenotes

The slender hands and claws *may have been adapted for digging small prey out of timber and rock crevices.*

Gigantoraptor

The tall crest *on top of the beak was very like that of a modern cassowary bird.*

Despite its small head, **Avimimus** *had a big brain for a dinosaur, and unusually large eyes.*

Citipati

Avimimus

Fossils show that Citipati *used its short "wings" to cover and protect its eggs in the nest.*

The long, sturdy legs of this animal *were adapted for fast running.*

of typically long-armed theropod dinosaurs called the maniraptorans, which also includes the birds. The maniraptorans probably all had feathery bodies and tails, and long feathers on their arms. Oviraptorosaurs also had bird-like, often toothless beaks, which they may have used to gather a wide range of food, including seeds, big insects, lizards, small mammals, and possibly even the eggs of other dinosaurs. They had two bony projections on the roof of the mouth that would have been ideal for cracking eggshells, so maybe they were egg thieves after all.

Arms and hands

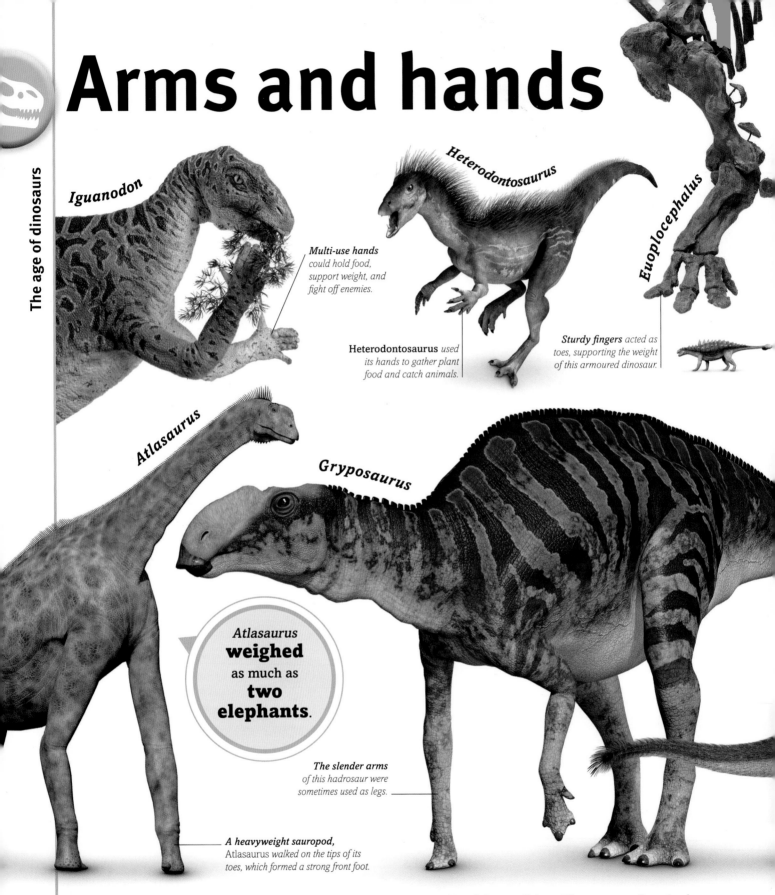

Iguanodon

Multi-use hands *could hold food, support weight, and fight off enemies.*

Heterodontosaurus

Heterodontosaurus *used its hands to gather plant food and catch animals.*

Euoplocephalus

Sturdy fingers *acted as toes, supporting the weight of this armoured dinosaur.*

Atlasaurus

Gryposaurus

Atlasaurus **weighed** as much as **two elephants**.

The slender arms *of this hadrosaur were sometimes used as legs.*

A heavyweight sauropod, Atlasaurus *walked on the tips of its toes, which formed a strong front foot.*

The arms and hands of dinosaurs evolved in different ways to perform a variety of tasks. Those of small plant-eaters were adapted for gathering food, but many, like *Iguanodon*, used their hands to support their weight. Bigger plant-eaters had very stout forelimbs that were specialized for walking. The arms of typical meat-eaters like the powerful *Dubreuillosaurus* were adapted for gripping struggling prey while the predator got to work with its jaws. They were short but strong, with sharp claws. Over time, some hunters, such as *Citipati* and

Sinornithosaurus

Carnotaurus

These tiny arms were useless for hunting but may have had other uses.

Citipati

Fossils of **Citipati** show it brooding eggs with its long, feathered arms.

Long feathers almost hide the sharp claws of this small, long-armed hunter.

Dubreuillosaurus

Most hunters had three-fingered hands with sharp claws.

Deinocheirus

The plant-eating **Deinocheirus** had huge hands, each with three clawed fingers that it probably used for defence.

GIANT ARMS

The enormous hands of this dinosaur earned it the name *Deinocheirus,* which is Greek for "terrible hand". The arms were 2.5 m (8 ft) long and ended in hands that were about 76 cm (2½ ft) long.

The three-fingered hand had huge, blunt claws.

Sinornithosaurus, developed much longer arms and hands. These were often used in the same way, but recent fossil evidence shows that they carried long feathers, almost like wings, and *Citipati* used these to shelter its eggs and young. Relatives of these animals had even longer feathered arms, and they became the first birds. By contrast, some very powerful hunters, including **Carnotaurus** and the tyrannosaurs, evolved very short arms and relied on their jaws to subdue prey.

PROTECTIVE WINGS
Seventy-five million years ago, the deserts of southern Mongolia were just as dry as they are today, with extensive sand dunes and few rivers. Despite this, they were home to several dinosaurs. They included the ostrich-like *Citipati* – famous among scientists for their amazing fossils, which show that these dinosaurs incubated their eggs like birds.

Like many other theropods, *Citipati* had long arms equipped with feathers similar to the flight feathers of bird wings. But *Citipati* clearly could not fly, because its "wings" were far too short. The feathers must have had another function, and several fossils found in the Gobi Desert show what that might have been. The animals are preserved crouching on top of clutches of eggs, with their arms spread out to the edges of the nest. In this position, their long feathers would have covered the eggs, keeping them warm or shading them from the scorching desert sunshine. But feathers could not protect *Citipati* and its eggs from whatever killed, buried, and preserved them as fossils beneath the desert sand.

Therizinosaurs

The beak-tipped jaws were adapted for eating leaves, which all therizinosaurs chewed using small cheek teeth.

At up to **11 m (36 ft)** long, *Therizinosaurus* was as **big** as a tyrannosaur.

Fossils of related species show simple feathers that were like flattened hairs, forming a fur-like coat.

Nothronychus **was the first therizinosaur** to be found in North America; the others have all been found in Mongolia and China.

Therizinosaurus

Nothronychus

A long neck helped Nothronychus *reach high into the trees to gather leaves; it stood up to 3.6 m (12 ft) tall.*

The body was bulkier than a typical theropod and the posture more upright.

Like all theropods, therizinosaurs stood on their hind legs, which were unusually short compared to their bodies.

The sword-like curved claws were about 1 m (3 ft) long and had sharp tips, making them effective weapons.

Sturdy, broad feet were adapted for supporting the animal's weight, and not for moving at speed.

Most theropods were sharp-toothed, agile hunters, but the therizinosaurs were different. Very few complete fossils have been found, but when paleontologists pieced together the evidence, therizinosaurs turned out to be unusual. They had beaked jaws, leaf-shaped cheek teeth, and bulky bodies, suggesting that they probably fed on plants instead of hunting prey. They were long-armed members of the maniraptorans – a group of theropods related to birds – and like them, were feathered. But the feathers seem to have been reduced to slender

Unusually, Falcarius had some pointed teeth in the front of its jaws that it may have used to catch small animals.

Falcarius

Alxasaurus   *Therizinosaurus*

Erlikosaurus

The jaws were lined with more than 100 small teeth, adapted for shredding leafy food.

Falcarius is the most primitive known therizinosaur; it lived about 126 million years ago.

Fossils of Enigmosaurus, meaning "riddle lizard", were unearthed in Mongolia.

Erlikosaurus *had long foot claws that may have helped it defend itself.*

Enigmosaurus

The tails of all therizinosaurs were relatively short.

Alxasaurus is named after the Alxa Desert of Mongolia, where its fossils were found in the early 1990s.

Alxasaurus

The arms probably had long feathers similar to those of birds.

Like all therizinosaurs, Enigmosaurus *had long arms and hands.*

filaments, making therizinosaurs like **Erlikosaurus** look as though they had dense fur. Their long arms had big hands equipped with huge claws – those of the giant **Therizinosaurus** are the longest claws of any known animal. The therizinosaurs may have used their claws to haul leafy branches within reach of their mouths. But they could also have used their claws as formidable weapons against predators. With their bulky bodies, therizinosaurs could not move quickly, so fighting may have been their best form of self-defence.

Sharp claws

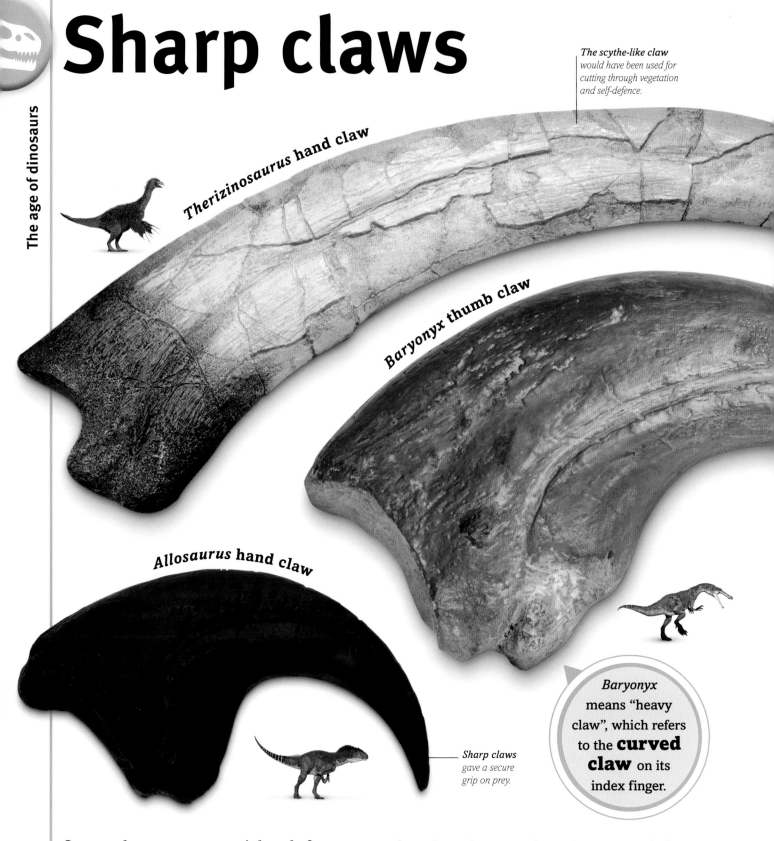

The scythe-like claw would have been used for cutting through vegetation and self-defence.

Therizinosaurus hand claw

Baryonyx thumb claw

Allosaurus hand claw

Sharp claws gave a secure grip on prey.

Baryonyx means "heavy claw", which refers to the **curved claw** on its index finger.

Strong claws were essential tools for most dinosaurs. Like many hunters, **Allosaurus** and **Baryonyx** used the claws on their forelimbs to seize prey, while **Deinonychus** had foot claws that were specialized for pinning prey to the ground. Most predators had strong but sharp foot claws that gave them the grip needed for running, and some of the smaller, bird-like hunters may have used their claws to climb trees. Gigantic four-footed plant-eaters such as **Apatosaurus** had stout claws that helped support their colossal weight, but they also may

Hypsilophodon toe claw

This plant-eater used its long sharp claw to get a good grip on the soft ground of the woodlands in which it likely lived.

Plateosaurus hand claws

Each hand had three claws for gathering food.

Oviraptor hand claw

Scientists think **Oviraptor** *may have used its hand claw to hold on to its prey.*

Iguanodon thumb spike

The thumb spike was used for defence.

Apatosaurus claw

The thumb on the pillar-like front legs ended in a stout claw, and may have been used for digging.

The fish-eating **Baryonyx** *would have used its large curved claw to seize slippery fish.*

Deinonychus toe claws

To keep it sharp, this large claw was held off the ground when running.

The smaller claws helped Deinonychus grip the ground.

FORMIDABLE CLAWS

The claws of the plant-eating *Therizinosaurus* were about 71 cm (28 in) long – the longest claws ever known. The points and edges of the claws would have been sharp enough to inflict serious injuries.

Therizinosaurus claw
71 cm (28 in)

| 0 cm (0 in) | 20 cm (8 in) | 40 cm (16 in) | 60 cm (24 in) | 80 cm (31 in) |

have used them to dig holes where they laid their eggs. **Plateosaurus** stood on its hind legs and used its front claws to gather food from trees or, more vitally, defend itself from predators. **Iguanodon** had a stout thumb spike, which it may have used against its enemies, while **Therizinosaurus** had astonishingly long claws on its forelimbs that would have been lethal weapons, ideal for defence against some of the most powerful predators that ever existed.

Dromaeosaurs

Buitreraptor

The body was probably covered with feathers, similar to those of modern birds.

The jaws of this big, South American hunter were unusually long, like a crocodile's.

Most dromaeosaurs had strong hands that they used to grab their prey.

Deinonychus

The *Velociraptor* depicted in the film ***Jurassic Park*** was based on *Deinonychus*.

The arms of Austroraptor were unusually short for a dromaeosaur, suggesting a different hunting technique.

Long, sharp claws on its hands ensured that Deinonychus kept a tight grip on its victims.

Sinornithosaurus

Many of these dinosaurs also had long feathers on their legs.

Long feathers on the arms were almost like wings, but not big enough for flight.

The most well-known lightweight hunters of the dinosaur age are the dromaeosaurs, often called raptor dinosaurs after animals like the small, agile *Velociraptor*. They were typically long-armed hunters with large claws on their hands. The second toe on each foot had an oversized, hooked claw that was held off the ground to keep it sharp. This specialized claw was probably used to pin prey to the ground, or even – in smaller types – to climb trees. Recent fossils found in China show that these dinosaurs were covered in feathers, and many had long,

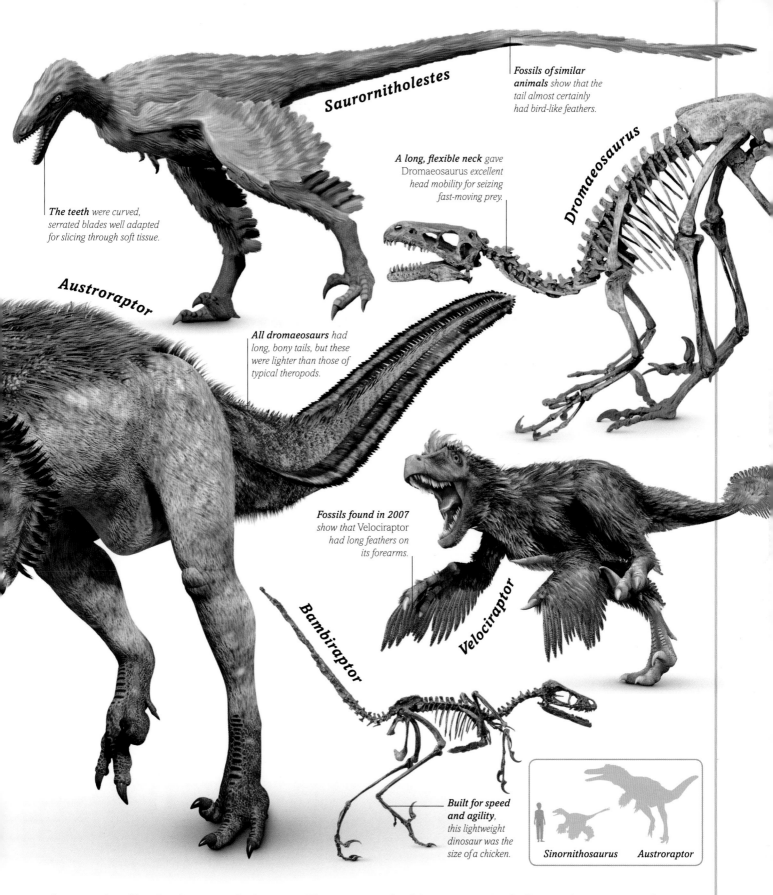

Saurornitholestes

Fossils of similar animals show that the tail almost certainly had bird-like feathers.

A long, flexible neck gave Dromaeosaurus excellent head mobility for seizing fast-moving prey.

Dromaeosaurus

The teeth were curved, serrated blades well adapted for slicing through soft tissue.

Austroraptor

All dromaeosaurs had long, bony tails, but these were lighter than those of typical theropods.

Fossils found in 2007 show that Velociraptor had long feathers on its forearms.

Bambiraptor

Velociraptor

Built for speed and agility, this lightweight dinosaur was the size of a chicken.

Sinornithosaurus   *Austroraptor*

almost wing-like feathers on their arms. They were closely related to the first birds, and the smallest ones – animals like **Sinornithosaurus** – would have looked very bird-like. Small dromaeosaurs would have preyed on big insects and small rat-like mammals, but we know that

the bigger ones, including *Velociraptor* and **Deinonychus**, attacked other dinosaurs. Some, such as **Buitreraptor** and the unusually large **Austroraptor**, had long snouts filled with pointed, conical teeth that were more suited to catching fish.

127

TOOTHED EAGLE
When the first fossils of *Velociraptor* were found in Mongolia in the 1920s, it was imagined as a scaly, lizard-like animal. But fossils of a closely related dinosaur discovered in nearby China show that *Velociraptor* would have looked more like a bird. A row of bumps on one of its forearm bones also shows that its arms carried long feathers very like those of a bird's wing.

Even the behaviour of *Velociraptor* was probably bird-like. Related dinosaurs laid their eggs in nests and sat on the eggs to keep them warm, using their "wings" to shelter them. *Velociraptor* almost certainly nested like this, perhaps in pairs, and while one of the pair brooded the eggs, the other would go hunting. Recent research into how *Velociraptor* hunted suggests that it ran after its prey and pounced on them like a flightless eagle, pinning animals to the ground with the special, enlarged claws on its feet. The hunter would then tear into its unlucky victim with its sharp-edged, serrated teeth, ripping it to pieces. It may even have taken some of the meat back to the nest for its mate.

DINOSAURS TAKE FLIGHT

Skin, scales, and feathers

Archaeopteryx

Long feathers on its extended arms almost certainly gave this Jurassic dinosaur the ability to fly.

Like a chicken, **Juravenator** had feathers on its body and scales on its legs.

Edmontonia

Juravenator

The furry body covering of this small theropod dinosaur was made up of simple, hair-like protofeathers.

Edmontosaurus skin fossil

This fossil shows that the skin of Edmontosaurus was protected by small scales.

Most extinct dinosaurs are known only from fossils of their bones and teeth but some fossils also preserve details of soft tissues, such as skin. They show that many large dinosaurs like the hadrosaur *Edmontosaurus* had scaly skin, and some, such as *Edmontonia*, had a type of armour formed from plates of bone (scutes) embedded in the skin. Amazing fossils discovered recently in China have revealed that many small theropod dinosaurs had feathers. Some, like *Sinosauropteryx*, had short, slender filaments,

Scute

The fossilized feathers of Caihong *include microscopic structures like the melanosomes that create iridescent feather colours in some modern birds.*

Caihong

This armoured dinosaur's scutes were spike-shaped, partly for defence but perhaps also for show.

The legs and belly of Edmontonia *were covered with scaly skin, similar to that of many modern reptiles.*

Psittacosaurus fossil

This fossil of an early relative of the horned dinosaur Triceratops *shows that its tail was covered with long quills.*

The dark patches on this fossil are the remains of a fuzzy body covering made up of protofeathers.

Sinosauropteryx fossil

COLOUR CODING

New research has revealed that the fossil feathers of animals like *Caihong* preserve the remains of melanosomes – structures inside cells that contain colour pigments. The size, shape, and arrangement of these melanosomes are related to their colour. So, by analysing fossil melanosomes, scientists may be able to reconstruct the colours of feathered dinosaurs.

| Rust | Brown | Grey | Black | Iridescent |

or protofeathers, resembling hair; these probably kept the animal warm, like the fur of a mammal. Others, including **Caihong**, had fully vaned feathers, like those of modern birds. Some of these feathers were longer, especially on the arms, which would have looked like short wings.

Microscopic analysis even indicates that some of the feathers were brightly coloured. All this new evidence shows that there is little difference between these extinct theropod dinosaurs and living birds, and supports the conclusion that birds are small, flying dinosaurs.

Feathered hunters

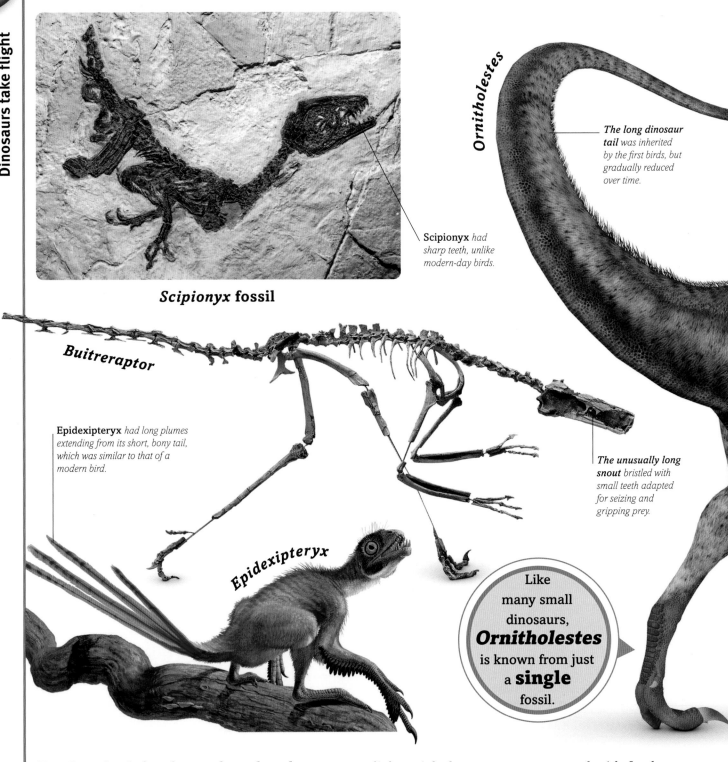

Ornitholestes

The long dinosaur tail was inherited by the first birds, but gradually reduced over time.

Scipionyx had sharp teeth, unlike modern-day birds.

Scipionyx fossil

Buitreraptor

Epidexipteryx had long plumes extending from its short, bony tail, which was similar to that of a modern bird.

The unusually long snout bristled with small teeth adapted for seizing and gripping prey.

Epidexipteryx

Like many small dinosaurs, ***Ornitholestes*** is known from just a **single** fossil.

For decades it has been clear that the skeletons of small, long-armed theropod dinosaurs like *Buitreraptor* are similar to that of the first known bird-like dinosaur, *Archaeopteryx*. More recent fossil evidence also shows that the bodies of many of these lightweight hunters were covered with feathers of some kind. This means that the only difference between these small dinosaurs and the first birds was the length of their arms and the nature of their feathers. At first sight a small, agile hunter with fuzzy feathers such as

Epidexipteryx   Ornitholestes

Shuvuuia

These animals *had relatively large brains and big eyes – both important for their flying descendants.*

Small hunters with feather-fringed tails *may have curled them over their sleeping bodies to keep warm.*

TINY SKULL

The skull of *Mononykus* was only slightly longer than a chicken egg. But its brain was quite large compared to its body size, suggesting that it was relatively intelligent. Its eyes were unusually big, indicating that they probably worked well in dim light, so it may have been most active at night or during the twilight of dawn and dusk.

5 cm (2 in) long
Chicken egg

The large eye socket suggests Mononykus had very good vision.

6 cm (2¼ in) long
Mononykus **skull**

Mononykus *was a small dinosaur from the plains of Mongolia.*

Mononykus
had a small skull.

Mononykus

The long feathers on the arms *were for show, and for protecting eggs and young, but in other animals they became adapted for flight.*

The short arms *had a single large claw that it could have used to dig insects out of dead wood.*

Mei long

A dense covering of body feathers *kept this animal warm.*

Mei long *had* **ornamental feathers** *on its legs as well as its arms.*

Ornitholestes might not seem very like a bird, but extend its arms and add some longer feathers, and it might look ready for take-off. The fossils of similar animals, like *Velociraptor*, show that they had long, bird-like feathers sprouting from their arms, and many also had feathery fans on their tails. A fossil of **Epidexipteryx** clearly shows four very long ornamental tail feathers. This type of feathering made small hunters such as **Mei long** look like short-winged pheasants or chickens, and if they were alive today we would instantly recognize them as flightless birds.

135

First up

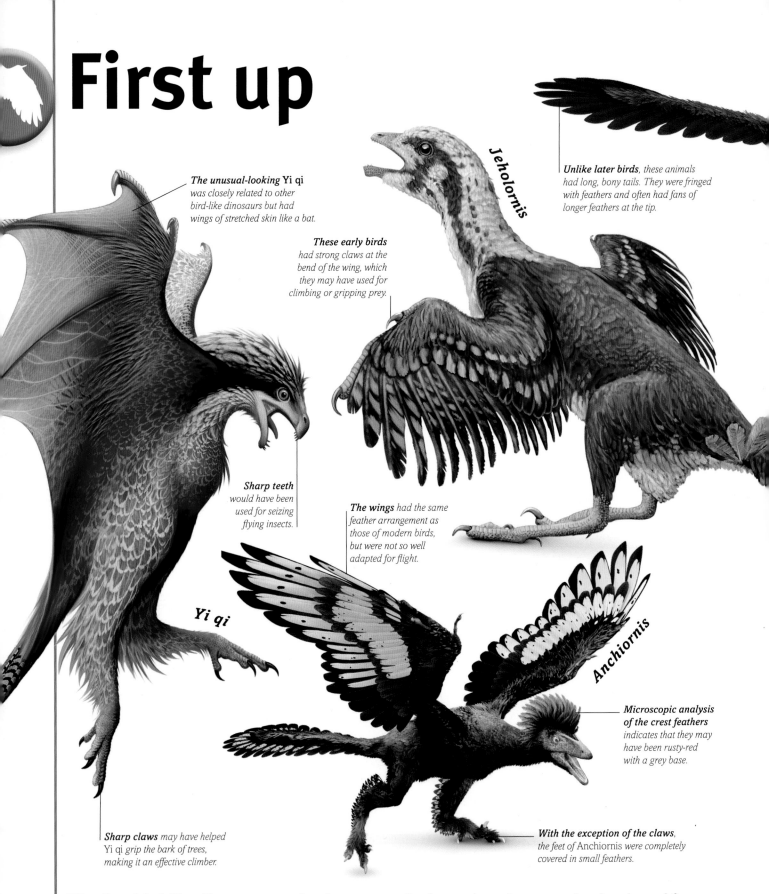

The unusual-looking Yi qi *was closely related to other bird-like dinosaurs but had wings of stretched skin like a bat.*

These early birds had strong claws at the bend of the wing, which they may have used for climbing or gripping prey.

Jeholornis

Unlike later birds, these animals had long, bony tails. They were fringed with feathers and often had fans of longer feathers at the tip.

Sharp teeth would have been used for seizing flying insects.

The wings had the same feather arrangement as those of modern birds, but were not so well adapted for flight.

Yi qi

Anchiornis

Microscopic analysis of the crest feathers indicates that they may have been rusty-red with a grey base.

Sharp claws may have helped Yi qi grip the bark of trees, making it an effective climber.

With the exception of the claws, the feet of Anchiornis were completely covered in small feathers.

The first bird-like dinosaurs evolved in the Jurassic Period at least 150 million years ago. They had toothed jaws and long, feather-fringed tails, just like many small non-flying hunters that lived at the time. They resemble birds because most of them had long feathery wings that were clearly adapted for some sort of flight. But we do not know how well they could fly. The wing feathers of animals like **Archaeopteryx** and **Jeholornis** are similar to those of modern birds, but their shoulder joints did not allow them to raise their wings

Archaeopteryx

The second toe had a hooked claw that was held off the ground to keep it sharp.

Archaeopteryx was the first known **bird-like dinosaur**.

One fossil of Jeholornis *shows a fan of ornamental feathers projecting from the base of the tail.*

Microraptor *had big eyes, which suggests it was active at night or lived in dense forest.*

Microraptor

The wing feathers *were about 20 cm (8 in) long, and may have helped it to glide from tree to tree.*

Fossils show *that the legs had long feathers that were similar to the wing feathers.*

This well-preserved fossil *clearly shows the bird-like feathers on its arms, legs, and tail.*

Microraptor fossil

Anchiornis   Microraptor

very high, and unlike modern birds they did not have big breastbones to anchor powerful flight muscles. Some like **Microraptor** almost certainly could not fly in the true sense. It is possible that they were mainly adapted for gliding from tree to tree, but the feet of **Jeholornis** and many others were far better suited to life on the ground. So we still do not know exactly how these animals took to the air. We just know that they had long, broad wings, which would have been of little use if they could not fly in some way.

TAKING OFF
In the Late Jurassic Period, 150 million years ago, the age of dinosaurs still had more than 80 million years to run. But already the first bird-like creatures were experimenting with flight. One of the earliest was *Archaeopteryx*, a crow-sized relative of agile hunters like *Velociraptor* that had particularly long arms with bird-like feathers. It was not exactly a bird, but it was close.

All the specimens of *Archaeopteryx* found so far lived in a region of Europe that was reduced to a group of dry islands surrounded by shallow seas. The islands seem to have had few trees, and *Archaeopteryx* probably ate small ground-living animals like lizards and insects. But its long, feathery wings must have been useful in some way. They may have helped it accelerate in pursuit of prey over the ground. It is also possible that, like modern chickens, it used them to fly up into tall shrubs to roost at night, out of reach of prowling hunters. It may have evolved in a region with taller trees, and used its wings to glide between them. We do not know – but one day another fossil may solve the riddle.

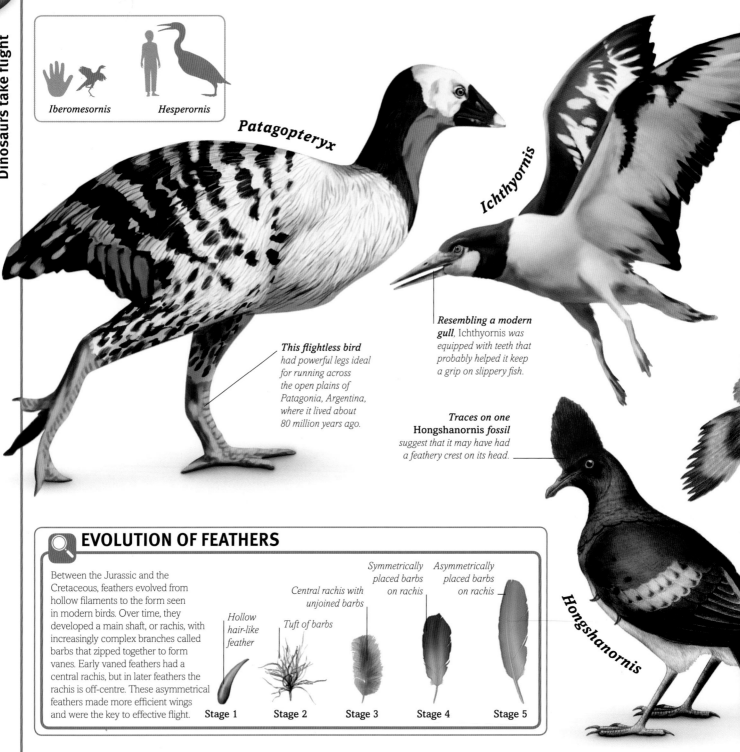

Early birds

Iberomesornis   Hesperornis

Patagopteryx

Ichthyornis

This flightless bird had powerful legs ideal for running across the open plains of Patagonia, Argentina, where it lived about 80 million years ago.

Resembling a modern gull, Ichthyornis was equipped with teeth that probably helped it keep a grip on slippery fish.

Traces on one Hongshanornis *fossil* suggest that it may have had a feathery crest on its head.

Hongshanornis

EVOLUTION OF FEATHERS

Between the Jurassic and the Cretaceous, feathers evolved from hollow filaments to the form seen in modern birds. Over time, they developed a main shaft, or rachis, with increasingly complex branches called barbs that zipped together to form vanes. Early vaned feathers had a central rachis, but in later feathers the rachis is off-centre. These asymmetrical feathers made more efficient wings and were the key to effective flight.

Hollow hair-like feather

Tuft of barbs

Central rachis with unjoined barbs

Symmetrically placed barbs on rachis

Asymmetrically placed barbs on rachis

Stage 1   Stage 2   Stage 3   Stage 4   Stage 5

In the Cretaceous Period, about 25 million years after *Archaeopteryx* made its first clumsy flight, the early bird-like dinosaurs started giving way to more modern-looking birds like *Confuciusornis*. This is one of the oldest short-tailed, toothless birds known, although it still had substantial wing claws. Like other birds of the same period, including the sparrow-sized **Iberomesornis** and the slightly bigger **Concornis**, it had a big breastbone for anchoring flight muscles; it must have been able to fly well. In time, birds like **Hongshanornis**

Hesperornis

Concornis **was about the same size** as a starling, but not as agile in the air.

To aid flight, *the wing feathers were asymmetrical, like those of modern birds.*

Confuciusornis

A male Confuciusornis *had two long tail streamers.*

Concornis

Hesperornis *was about 1.8 m (6 ft) long.*

Iberomesornis

The wings *of this enormous toothed seabird were reduced to tiny stumps, so it could not fly.*

Strong claws and a back-pointing toe *on each foot allowed Iberomesornis to perch on branches.*

Hesperornis *swam using its large webbed feet.*

became more specialized for flight, with stronger skeletons to resist flight stresses. Many still had small teeth, especially fish-eating seabirds like **Ichthyornis**, which lived about 90 million years ago. But others had abandoned them in favour of beaks, and by the Late Cretaceous, about

70 million years ago, many modern-type birds were flying over the heads of the giant dinosaurs. Some birds, including **Patagopteryx**, had given up flight to live like ostriches, while the flightless **Hesperornis** hunted underwater like a giant cormorant.

Giant birds

Gallinuloides   Dromornis

At 3 m (10 ft) tall, *Dromornis* was the **largest flightless bird** that ever existed.

Dromornis

Terror birds *had huge, hooked beaks for killing and tearing the flesh of their victims.*

Phorusrhacos

Phorusrhacos *had a very flexible neck that allowed it to strike quickly at prey.*

The massive legs *of* Dromornis *supported its colossal weight – it weighed 10 times as much as a human.*

This fossil *shows that birds very similar to modern chickens were living in North America 48 million years ago.*

Sharp claws *were used to pin struggling prey to the ground as the bird prepared to kill and eat it.*

Gallinuloides fossil

Birds were the only dinosaurs to survive the mass extinction that wiped out their giant relatives 66 million years ago. They evolved to form many new types that are still with us today, including owls, ducks, and penguins. By about 40 million years ago, most of the familiar bird groups had appeared, but there were also a few very unfamiliar birds, including giant, flightless predators known as "terror birds". They included ***Phorusrhacos*** and ***Titanis***. Both were more than 2 m (8 ft) tall and had hooked beaks and huge claws for

Teratornis

Hundreds of skeletons of this ice-age, vulture-like predator have been found in sticky tar deposits in California, USA.

Osteodontornis

The beak was lined with bony, tooth-like serrations, perfect for catching slippery fish.

Argentavis

This bird of prey weighed five times as much as the very similar Andean condor – one of the largest modern flying birds.

Titanis

Also known as Diatryma, this giant flightless bird may have eaten leaves and shoots, or been good at cracking open large seeds and nuts.

Long legs allowed Titanis to run at speeds of more than 48 km/h (30 mph) – fast enough to catch most small animals.

Icadyptes

Icadyptes had a much longer, more pointed beak than modern penguins.

Gastornis

Fossil footprints suggest that the three-toed feet were about 40 cm (16 in) long.

ripping apart prey on the open plains of North and South America. They were among the most powerful predators of their time. Another flightless giant, the Australian **Dromornis**, probably ate plants, and the same may apply to the much earlier **Gastornis**. Meanwhile, some airborne birds were also giants. **Argentavis**, which soared above the plains of Argentina more than 5 million years ago, was a colossal, vulture-like bird of prey with an 8 m (26 ft) wingspan, and probably the largest flying bird that has ever lived.

HIGH-SPEED KILLER
With its long legs and massive hooked beak, *Kelenken* was one of the fastest, most powerful predators of its era. The biggest of the ferocious "terror birds", it hunted in the open plains of Patagonia, South America, about 15 million years ago. Its main prey were probably small mammals, but it may have had the speed and strength to hunt bigger victims.

Discovered in 2006, the virtually intact fossil skull of *Kelenken* was 71 cm (28 in) long, making it the biggest bird skull ever found. Its enormous, immensely strong hooked beak would have been like that of a gigantic eagle, and *Kelenken* probably used it in the same way to rip larger prey to pieces; it would have swallowed small animals whole. About 3 m (10 ft) tall,

Kelenken had long, muscular legs that ensured it could outrun most of its victims, and it probably caught and even killed them by seizing and gripping them with its claws. It was so powerful that it may have driven other hunters off the open plains and into the forests, where its height would have made it a less effective predator.

PTEROSAURS

Early pterosaurs

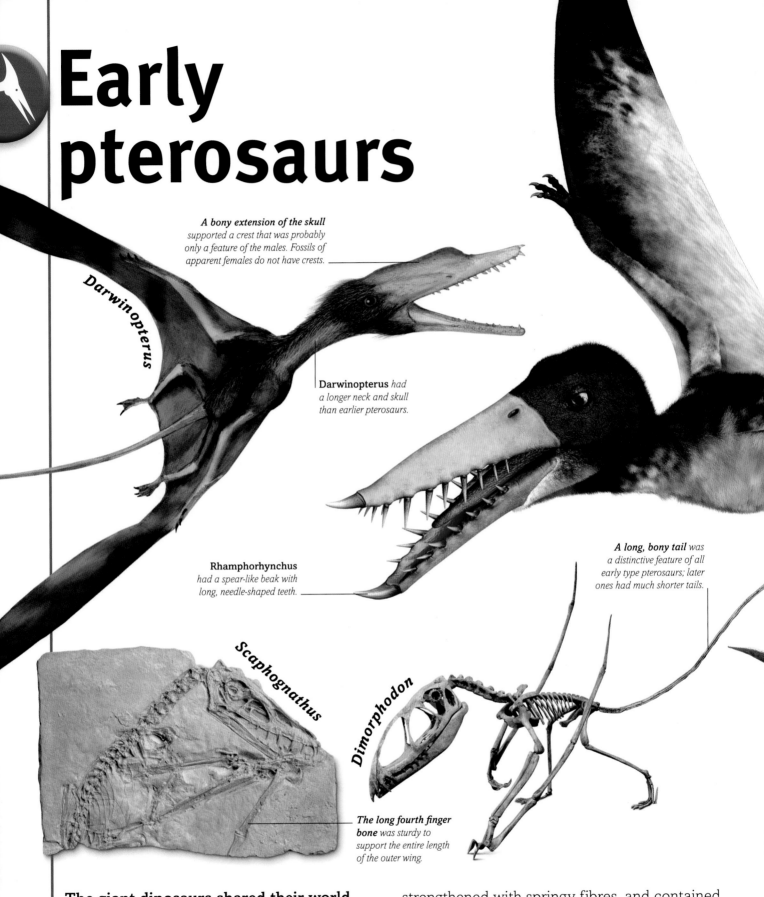

Darwinopterus

A bony extension of the skull supported a crest that was probably only a feature of the males. Fossils of apparent females do not have crests.

Darwinopterus had a longer neck and skull than earlier pterosaurs.

Rhamphorhynchus had a spear-like beak with long, needle-shaped teeth.

A long, bony tail was a distinctive feature of all early type pterosaurs; later ones had much shorter tails.

Scaphognathus

Dimorphodon

The long fourth finger bone was sturdy to support the entire length of the outer wing.

The giant dinosaurs shared their world with close relatives called pterosaurs – flying reptiles that flew on wings of stretched skin. Their wings were similar to those of bats, but supported by the bones of just one hugely elongated finger. They were strengthened with springy fibres, and contained sheets of muscle that continually adjusted the wing's shape to make it work as efficiently as possible. Pterosaurs had small, furry, and light bodies, excellent eyesight, and relatively big brains. The earliest ones found so far –

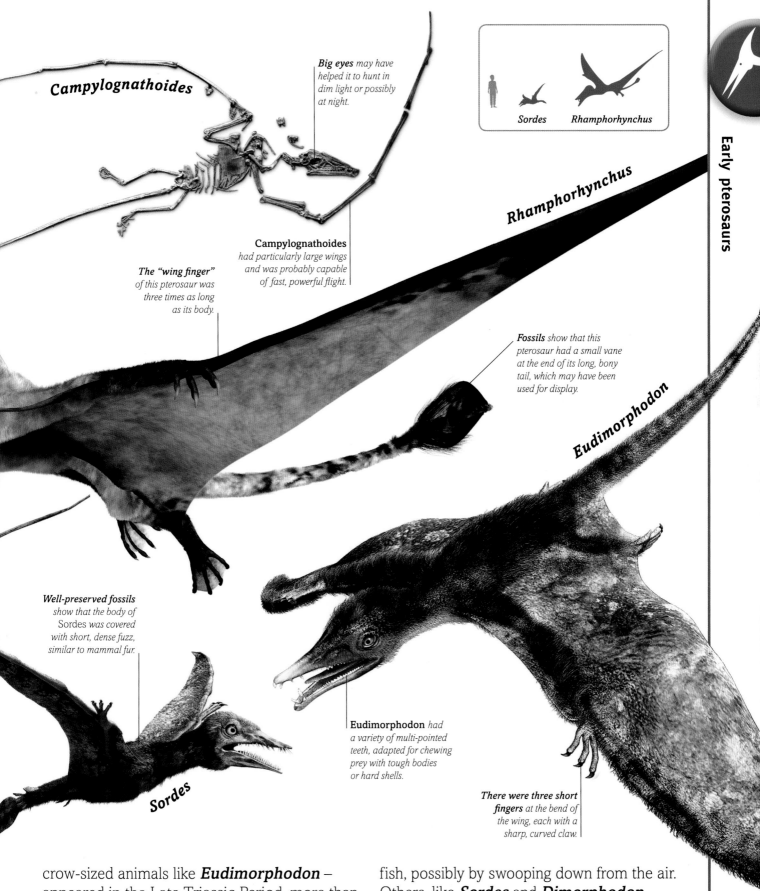

Campylognathoides

Big eyes *may have helped it to hunt in dim light or possibly at night.*

Campylognathoides *had particularly large wings and was probably capable of fast, powerful flight.*

The "wing finger" *of this pterosaur was three times as long as its body.*

Sordes   Rhamphorhynchus

Rhamphorhynchus

Fossils *show that this pterosaur had a small vane at the end of its long, bony tail, which may have been used for display.*

Eudimorphodon

Well-preserved fossils *show that the body of Sordes was covered with short, dense fuzz, similar to mammal fur.*

Eudimorphodon *had a variety of multi-pointed teeth, adapted for chewing prey with tough bodies or hard shells.*

Sordes

There were three short fingers *at the bend of the wing, each with a sharp, curved claw.*

crow-sized animals like **Eudimorphodon** – appeared in the Late Triassic Period, more than 210 million years ago. They had short necks and long, bony tails. Most also had jaws armed with a variety of sharp teeth to suit their diet. Some, such as **Rhamphorhynchus** caught fish, possibly by swooping down from the air. Others, like **Sordes** and **Dimorphodon**, probably fed mainly on insects and other small animals that they caught on the ground, or while climbing trees using their sharp wing claws.

149

Later pterosaurs

Discovered in Brazil in 2013, this mid-sized pterosaur had a spectacular head crest.

The wingspan was more than 3 m (10 ft).

Caupedactylus

Like most pterosaurs, Pteranodon had three mobile fingers at the bend of each wing.

More than **1,200** fossil specimens make *Pteranodon* the **best-known** pterosaur.

The long necks of later pterosaurs made it easy for them to snatch prey off the ground.

Pterosaurs had excellent vision, like birds, and highly developed flight control centres in the brain.

Elanodactylus

Ludodactylus

Tapejara   Pteranodon

During the Jurassic Period, about 166 million years ago, pterosaurs with a new body plan started appearing. They had longer necks, shorter tails, and were also better adapted to life on the ground – evidence from fossil footprints shows that many of them, including **Tapejara** and **Elanodactylus**, regularly walked on all fours, with their outer wings folded out of the way. Some pterosaurs were probably agile enough to hunt like this. Others, like **Pteranodon** and **Cearadactylus**, seem to have hunted at sea – they were probably

150

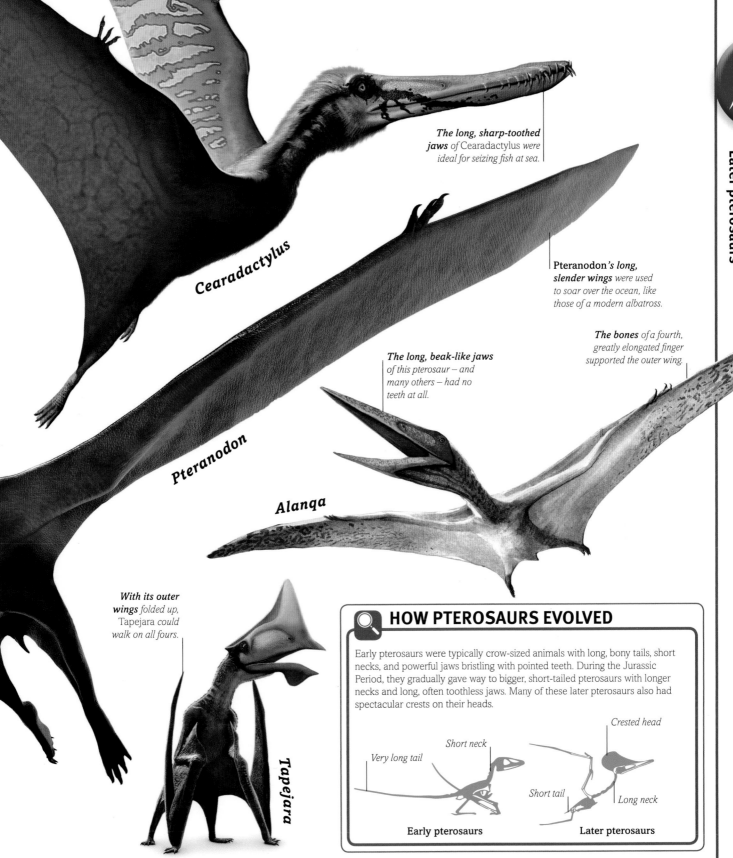

The long, sharp-toothed jaws of Cearadactylus were ideal for seizing fish at sea.

Cearadactylus

Pteranodon's long, slender wings were used to soar over the ocean, like those of a modern albatross.

The bones of a fourth, greatly elongated finger supported the outer wing.

The long, beak-like jaws of this pterosaur – and many others – had no teeth at all.

Pteranodon

Alanqa

With its outer wings folded up, Tapejara could walk on all fours.

Tapejara

HOW PTEROSAURS EVOLVED

Early pterosaurs were typically crow-sized animals with long, bony tails, short necks, and powerful jaws bristling with pointed teeth. During the Jurassic Period, they gradually gave way to bigger, short-tailed pterosaurs with longer necks and long, often toothless jaws. Many of these later pterosaurs also had spectacular crests on their heads.

Very long tail

Short neck

Crested head

Short tail

Long neck

Early pterosaurs

Later pterosaurs

able to swim on the ocean surface like seabirds and dive briefly below to catch fish. Many of these later pterosaurs were giants compared to the earlier ones. *Pteranodon* had a wingspan of more than 7 m (23 ft), and the biggest of all – *Quetzalcoatlus* and *Hatzegopteryx* – were the size of small aircraft, with wingspans of 10 m (33 ft) or more. These were the largest flying animals that ever lived, and all the evidence suggests that they were excellent fliers, able to cover vast distances by soaring on rising air currents like gigantic vultures.

PROWLING PREDATOR
The smaller dinosaurs that lived in North America 70 million years ago often fell prey to tyrannosaurs, but they also faced danger from another direction – the air. High above them, the skies were patrolled by *Quetzalcoatlus*, a gigantic pterosaur that would have soared in circles on rising air currents like a huge bird of prey, watching for a chance to seize a meal.

Quetzalcoatlus was superbly adapted for flight, and had excellent eyesight for targeting prey from long range. But it did not have powerful claws for seizing prey from the air. So, it probably landed first, folded up its long outer wings, and stalked on all fours through the undergrowth in search of food. As tall as a giraffe, *Quetzalcoatlus* could stand with its head well clear of any bushes or small trees. Its long neck and jaws also gave it a very long reach, so it could ambush animals from cover before they knew they were being watched. Since *Quetzalcoatlus* lacked teeth or a hooked beak, it could not tear prey apart, but it was big enough to swallow dinosaurs like this baby titanosaur whole.

Colourful crests

Well-preserved fossils *show that the crest of a Pterodactylus was made entirely of springy cartilage and skin.*

Pterodactylus

Pterodactylus was the **first fossil pterosaur** known to science.

The crest of Thalassodromeus contained a thin sheet of bone.

This pterosaur *had a bony crest covered with skin that may have been brightly coloured.*

Thalassodromeus

Tupuxuara

The heads of many later pterosaurs had spectacular crests that were almost certainly for display to rivals and potential breeding partners. The crests of *Tupandactylus* and *Nyctosaurus* were huge but lightweight structures made of skin or horn supported by slender bony struts. The smaller crest of *Thalassodromeus* was based on a thin, lightweight plate of bone, while the crests of other species, including *Pterodactylus*, were made entirely of soft tissue. Pterosaur

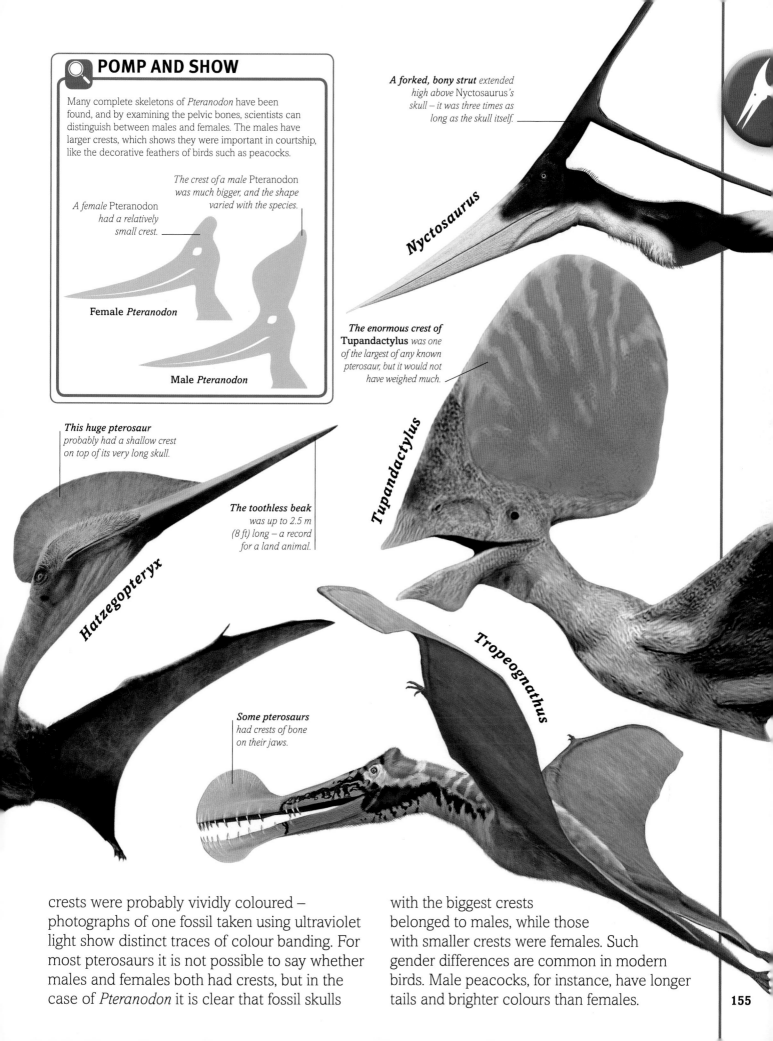

A forked, bony strut extended high above Nyctosaurus's skull – it was three times as long as the skull itself.

Nyctosaurus

The enormous crest of **Tupandactylus** *was one of the largest of any known pterosaur, but it would not have weighed much.*

Tupandactylus

This huge pterosaur probably had a shallow crest on top of its very long skull.

The toothless beak was up to 2.5 m (8 ft) long – a record for a land animal.

Hatzegopteryx

Tropeognathus

Some pterosaurs had crests of bone on their jaws.

crests were probably vividly coloured – photographs of one fossil taken using ultraviolet light show distinct traces of colour banding. For most pterosaurs it is not possible to say whether males and females both had crests, but in the case of *Pteranodon* it is clear that fossil skulls with the biggest crests belonged to males, while those with smaller crests were females. Such gender differences are common in modern birds. Male peacocks, for instance, have longer tails and brighter colours than females.

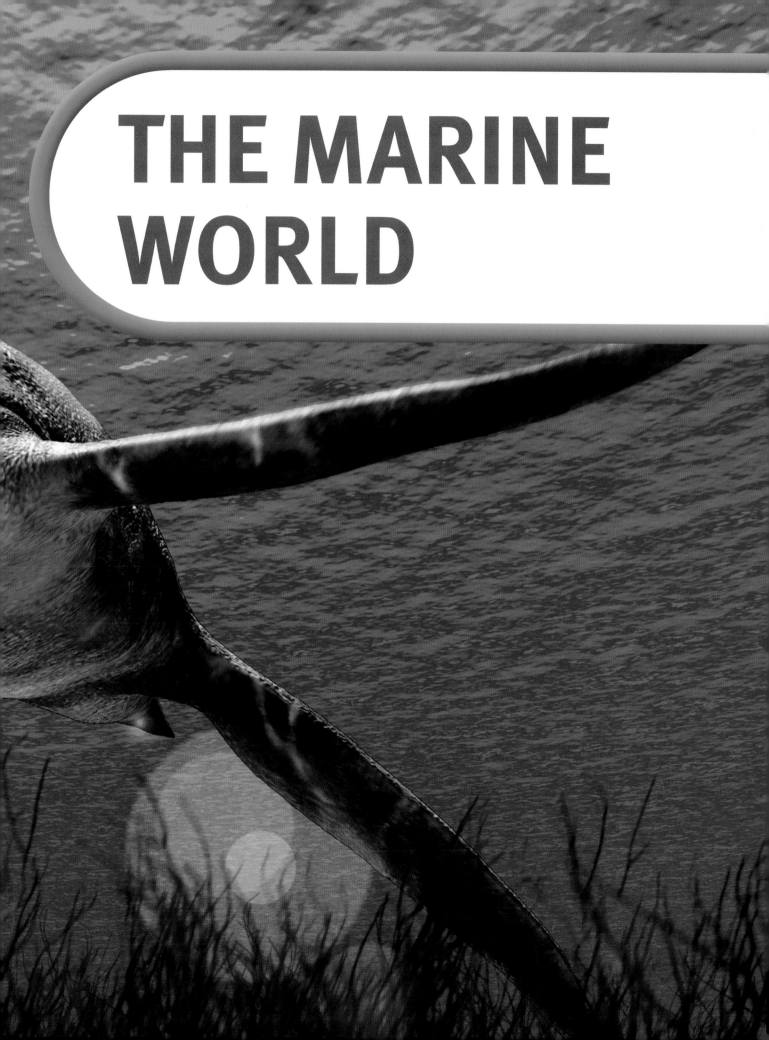

THE MARINE WORLD

Life in Mesozoic seas

This giant fish had mesh-like plates at the back of its mouth for sifting tiny drifting animals from the water.

Ammonite

The coiled shell protected the ammonite's soft body.

The shell was more than 5 cm (2 in) across.

This crab lived in warm, shallow seas about 80 million years ago.

Crab fossil

Leedsichthys

Sea snail fossil

This fossil shows the protective spiral shell made of hard chalky minerals absorbed from seawater.

LARGEST FISH

Leedsichthys
16.5 m (54 ft)

Longer than a school bus, and with a weight to match, *Leedsichthys* was one of the largest fish that has ever lived.

Bus 11 m (36 ft)

The Paleozoic Era – the age of ancient life – ended 252 million years ago with a devastating mass extinction of life. This event was so extreme that it destroyed about 96 per cent of all marine species. During the centuries that followed – the earliest years of the Mesozoic age of dinosaurs – the oceans would have been almost lifeless. But some animals survived and started to multiply, taking advantage of all the empty space. It took about 5 million years for the real recovery to begin, as the surviving marine animals evolved into

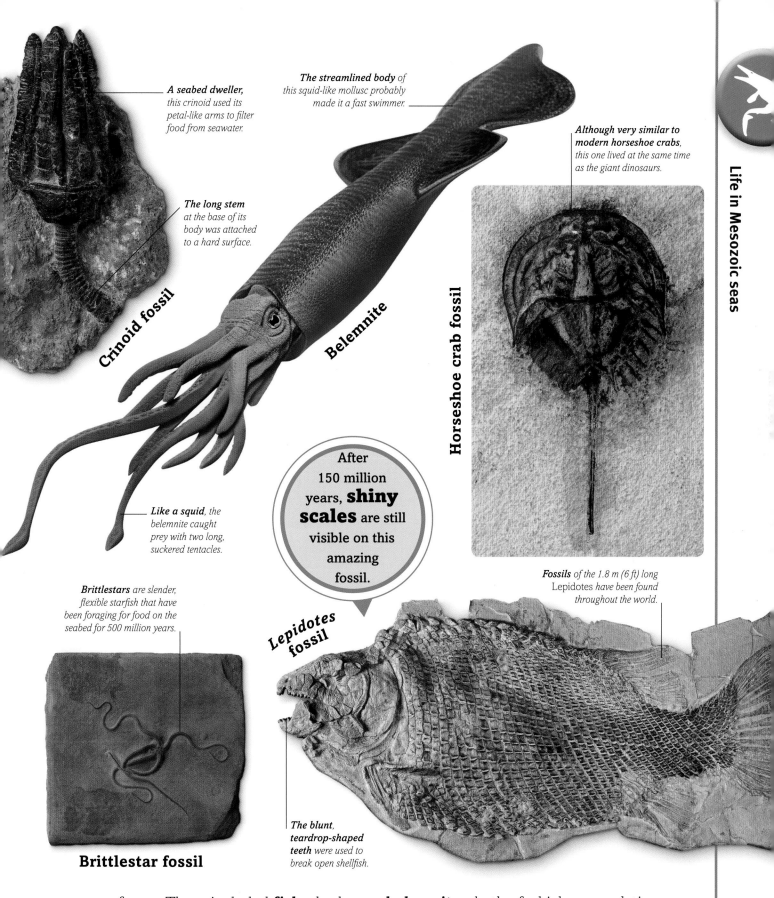

A seabed dweller, this crinoid used its petal-like arms to filter food from seawater.

The long stem at the base of its body was attached to a hard surface.

Crinoid fossil

The streamlined body of this squid-like mollusc probably made it a fast swimmer.

Belemnite

Like a squid, the belemnite caught prey with two long, suckered tentacles.

Although very similar to modern horseshoe crabs, this one lived at the same time as the giant dinosaurs.

Horseshoe crab fossil

After 150 million years, **shiny scales** are still visible on this amazing fossil.

Fossils of the 1.8 m (6 ft) long Lepidotes have been found throughout the world.

Brittlestars are slender, flexible starfish that have been foraging for food on the seabed for 500 million years.

Lepidotes fossil

The blunt, teardrop-shaped teeth were used to break open shellfish.

Brittlestar fossil

many new forms. These included **fish**, sharks, and marine reptiles, as well as invertebrates such as shelled molluscs, **crabs**, and **starfish**. Hard-shelled invertebrates in particular were common and have been fossilized in large numbers. They included **ammonites** and **belemnites**, both of which were relatives of squid. They perished in the mass extinction that ended the Mesozoic Era and destroyed the giant dinosaurs. But other types of sea creature survived and still flourish in the world's oceans.

Early marine reptiles

Unusually, this broad-mouthed reptile seems to have been a herbivore that fed on seaweed, like a modern marine iguana.

Guanlingsaurus

The head was long and flat with very powerful jaws, like the head of a modern crocodile.

The long teeth interlocked to trap fish and other slippery prey.

Like all ichthyosaurs, **Guanlingsaurus** *had a sleek, fish-like body adapted for speed through the water.*

Nothosaurus probably came ashore to **give birth** on beaches, like a **seal**.

Henodus

Henodus *had a protective shell made of plates of bone.*

The fish and other sea animals that lived during the time of the dinosaurs were preyed on by reptiles that were specially adapted for life in the oceans. These reptiles started becoming common in the seas about 245 million years ago, in the Triassic Period, and rapidly evolved a variety of adaptations for eating different kinds of food. Four-legged placodonts like **Placodus** searched the seabed for hard-shelled clams and similar shellfish, and other reptiles including **Atopodentatus** grazed on seaweed.

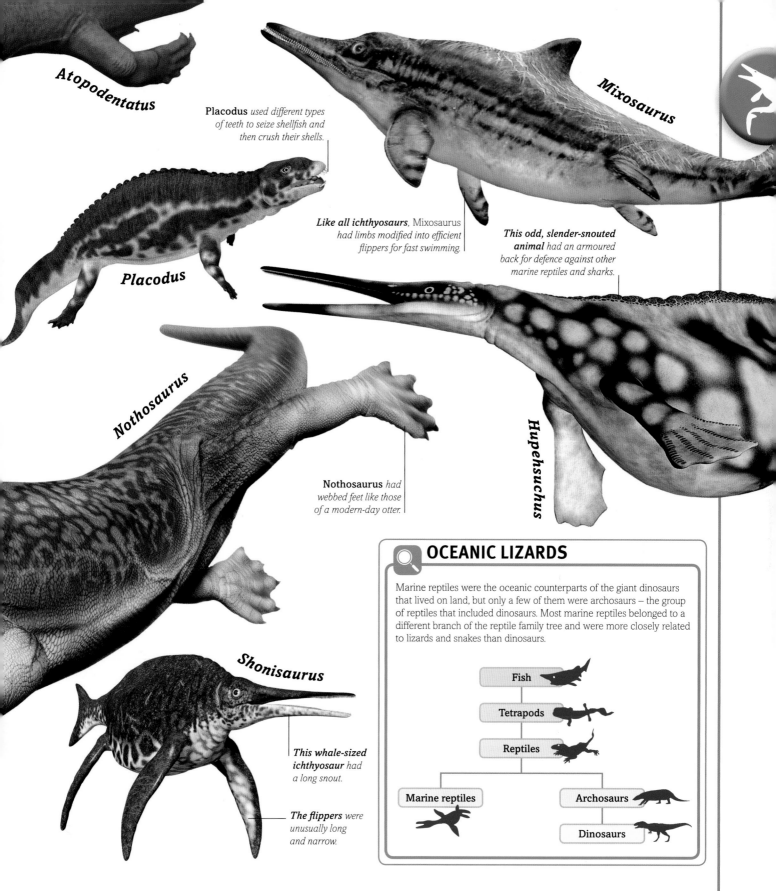

Atopodentatus

Mixosaurus

Placodus *used different types of teeth to seize shellfish and then crush their shells.*

Like all ichthyosaurs, Mixosaurus had limbs modified into efficient flippers for fast swimming.

This odd, slender-snouted animal *had an armoured back for defence against other marine reptiles and sharks.*

Placodus

Nothosaurus

Hupehsuchus

Nothosaurus *had webbed feet like those of a modern-day otter.*

Shonisaurus

This whale-sized ichthyosaur *had a long snout.*

The flippers *were unusually long and narrow.*

🔍 OCEANIC LIZARDS

Marine reptiles were the oceanic counterparts of the giant dinosaurs that lived on land, but only a few of them were archosaurs – the group of reptiles that included dinosaurs. Most marine reptiles belonged to a different branch of the reptile family tree and were more closely related to lizards and snakes than dinosaurs.

| Fish |
| Tetrapods |
| Reptiles |

| Marine reptiles | | Archosaurs |
| | | Dinosaurs |

Equipped with sharp-pointed teeth, the crocodile-like **Nothosaurus** preyed on other marine animals as well as fish. Most of these early marine reptiles had legs and probably lived partly on the shore, like seals. But the dolphin-like ichthyosaurs – animals like

Mixosaurus and **Shonisaurus** – were fully adapted to live permanently at sea, even though they had to breathe air. Their streamlined bodies and powerful tails were similar to those of sharks, enabling them to swim very fast in pursuit of fish.

Flippers and tails

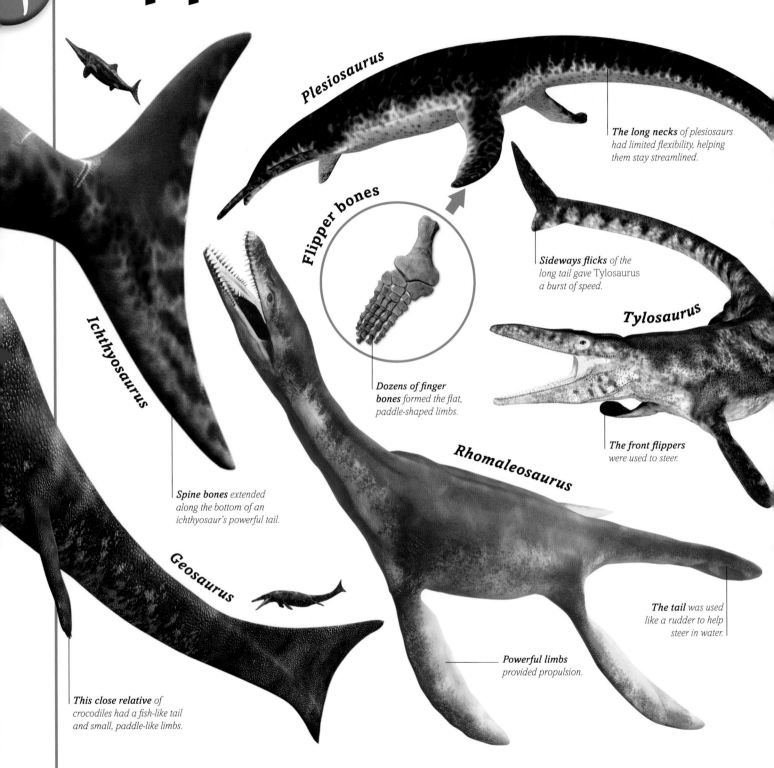

Plesiosaurus

The long necks of plesiosaurs had limited flexibility, helping them stay streamlined.

Flipper bones

Sideways flicks of the long tail gave Tylosaurus a burst of speed.

Tylosaurus

Ichthyosaurus

Dozens of finger bones formed the flat, paddle-shaped limbs.

The front flippers were used to steer.

Rhomaleosaurus

Spine bones extended along the bottom of an ichthyosaur's powerful tail.

The tail was used like a rudder to help steer in water.

Geosaurus

Powerful limbs provided propulsion.

This close relative of crocodiles had a fish-like tail and small, paddle-like limbs.

Many kinds of prehistoric reptile gave up life on land to live in the sea. Just as marine mammals like seals and whales would do later, they adapted to life in water by becoming streamlined and slippery and using their limbs as flippers. **Nothosaurus** had paddle-like, webbed feet for swimming, but it could also haul itself onto land to breed, as seals do. Other marine reptiles were fully aquatic and probably more agile in the sea. **Plesiosaurus** and its shorter-necked relative **Rhomaleosaurus** propelled themselves through water by rowing

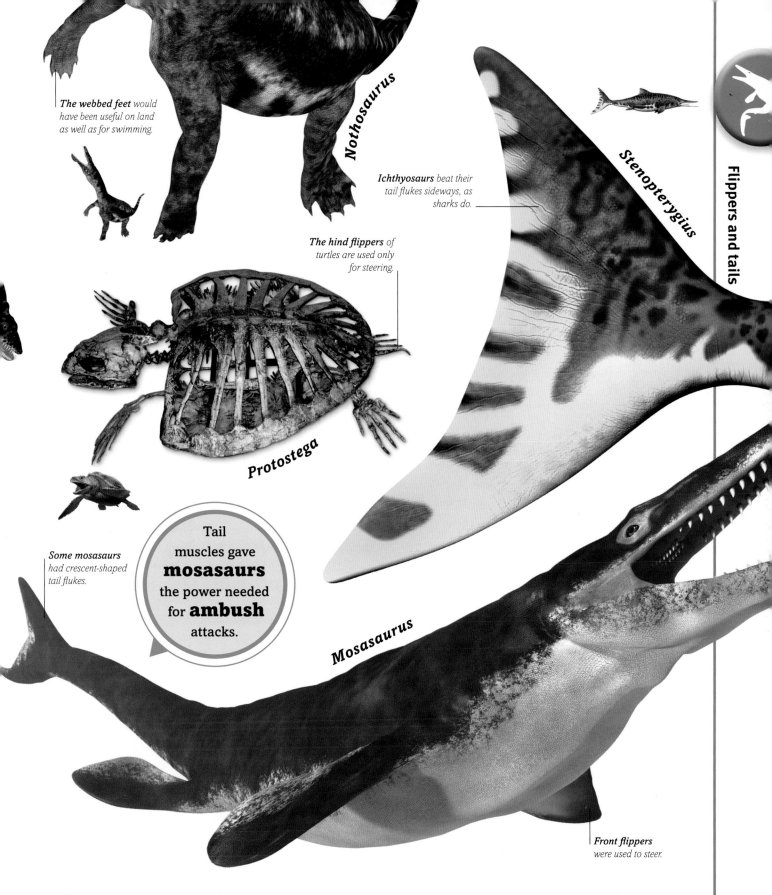

The webbed feet would have been useful on land as well as for swimming.

Nothosaurus

Ichthyosaurs beat their tail flukes sideways, as sharks do.

Stenopterygius

The hind flippers of turtles are used only for steering.

Protostega

Tail muscles gave **mosasaurs** the power needed for **ambush** attacks.

Some mosasaurs had crescent-shaped tail flukes.

Mosasaurus

Front flippers were used to steer.

or flapping their wing-like flippers. Whether they used all four for propulsion, or just the front ones for propulsion and rear pair for steering (like turtles), is unclear. The fastest swimmers of the reptile world were ichthyosaurs, such as **Ichthyosaurus** and **Stenopterygius**. They beat their shark-like tail flukes sideways for thrust and steered with their flippers. Early mosasaurs had flattened, crocodile-like tails that they swept from side to side to drive themselves through water. Later ones like **Mosasaurus** evolved tail flukes for greater efficiency.

163

Giant marine reptiles

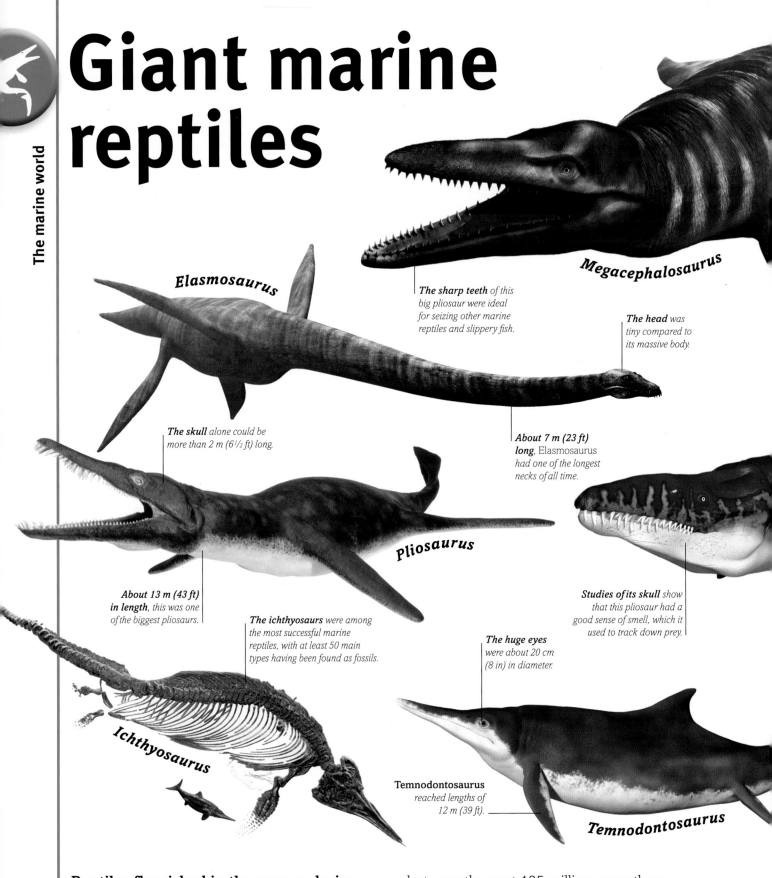

Megacephalosaurus

Elasmosaurus

The sharp teeth of this big pliosaur were ideal for seizing other marine reptiles and slippery fish.

The head was tiny compared to its massive body.

The skull alone could be more than 2 m (6½ ft) long.

About 7 m (23 ft) long, Elasmosaurus had one of the longest necks of all time.

Pliosaurus

About 13 m (43 ft) in length, this was one of the biggest pliosaurs.

The ichthyosaurs were among the most successful marine reptiles, with at least 50 main types having been found as fossils.

Studies of its skull show that this pliosaur had a good sense of smell, which it used to track down prey.

The huge eyes were about 20 cm (8 in) in diameter.

Ichthyosaurus

Temnodontosaurus reached lengths of 12 m (39 ft).

Temnodontosaurus

Reptiles flourished in the oceans during the Triassic Period. But about 200 million years ago, the Triassic Period came to an end with a mass extinction that destroyed many of the spectacular reptiles that had ruled the seas. The survivors took a long time to recover, but over the next 135 million years they evolved into some of the most powerful predators that have ever existed. Some, like **Dakosaurus**, resembled crocodiles but were specialized for life at sea. **Ichthyosaurus** and its giant relative **Temnodontosaurus** were

The powerful jaws were armed with sharp, crocodile-like teeth for seizing other marine reptiles, including smaller mosasaurs.

Dakosaurus's deep skull and teeth were like those of Tyrannosaurus.

Dakosaurus

About 10 m (33 ft) in length, this pliosaur flapped its four long, wing-like flippers to "fly" through water.

The first *Mosasaurus* **skull fossil** was discovered as long ago as 1764.

Liopleurodon

Mosasaurus had a long, flexible body, similar to snakes.

Mosasaurus

Ichthyosaurs had streamlined bodies and swam like sharks, using their powerful tail fins.

Mosasaurs swam by flexing their long bodies and tails, like crocodiles.

COLOSSAL REPTILES

Growing to at least 15 m (49 ft) long, mosasaurs were among the biggest marine reptiles. Like snakes, some mosasaurs had double-hinged jaws and flexible skulls that enabled them to swallow prey whole.

more like the reptile equivalents of dolphins. But the real marine giants were the long-necked reptiles known as plesiosaurs, which included **Elasmosaurus**, as well as the short-necked, fearsome pliosaurs like **Liopleurodon**, and the massive mosasaurs. Some marine reptiles had jaws that were far bigger than those of the deadly dinosaur *Tyrannosaurus*. All these marine reptiles were wiped out 66 million years ago in the mass extinction that killed the giant dinosaurs.

AMBUSH HUNTER
Some of the most deadly hunters that have ever existed lurked in the oceans during the Mesozoic Era. They included the pliosaurs – massive-jawed animals that were specialized for hunting big, powerful prey, including other marine reptiles. *Liopleurodon* was typical of these oceanic predators. About 7 m (23 ft) long and armed with huge, spike-shaped teeth, it had no predators.

Liopleurodon lived in the Late Jurassic oceans more than 163 million years ago. It was related to the long-necked plesiosaurs like the ones seen here, but that did not stop it from hunting them. Both these species drove themselves through the water with their long flippers. Experiments using swimming robots have shown that this could have given them tremendous acceleration. *Liopleurodon* may have used this speed as a part of its hunting strategy – lying in wait in the gloomy depths before surging to seize its prey and ripping it apart, although it could probably swallow this plesiosaur whole. A successful, formidable predator, *Liopleurodon* existed for nearly 10 million years.

THE RISE OF MAMMALS

A new world

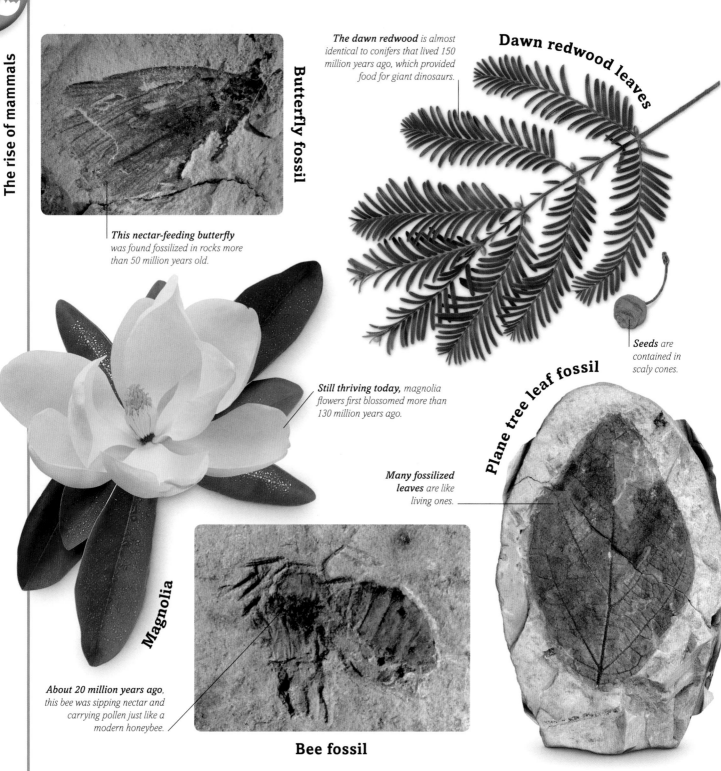

Butterfly fossil

This nectar-feeding butterfly was found fossilized in rocks more than 50 million years old.

The dawn redwood is almost identical to conifers that lived 150 million years ago, which provided food for giant dinosaurs.

Dawn redwood leaves

Seeds are contained in scaly cones.

Still thriving today, magnolia flowers first blossomed more than 130 million years ago.

Magnolia

Plane tree leaf fossil

Many fossilized leaves are like living ones.

About 20 million years ago, this bee was sipping nectar and carrying pollen just like a modern honeybee.

Bee fossil

During most of the Mesozoic age of dinosaurs there were no colourful, fragrant flowers to attract insects. The plant world was dominated by the green leaves of ferns, palm-like cycads, and conifer trees. The earliest known flowering plants date from about 140 million years ago. Most of their flowers were small and pollinated by the wind, like grass flowers. But by about 100 million years ago many had big, vibrant flowers like those of **early magnolias** and ***Archaeanthus***, and by the time the dinosaurs were wiped out, the world had

Florissantia fossil

Formed 49 million years ago, this fossil has traces of structures that produced sugary nectar.

The crushed exoskeleton of this 50-million-year-old beetle still glitters as it did when alive.

Giant winged ant fossil

Every detail of this queen ant has been preserved in a fossil that is about 47 million years old.

Archaeanthus

These bright petals would have attracted early pollen-feeding beetles.

Jewel beetle fossil

Still around today, **jewel beetles** date back to about 150 million years ago.

Water chestnut

The spiky fruit of water chestnuts provided food for early Stone-Age people.

been transformed. The following Cenozoic Era saw an increase in plants with showy, nectar-bearing, and possibly fragrant flowers like those of **Florissantia**. They evolved alongside nectar-feeding insects, including **bees** and **butterflies**. These insects transferred pollen from flower to flower much more efficiently than the wind, enabling the plants to set seed more easily. This meant that the Cenozoic – the age of mammals – was probably far more colourful than all previous ages, and buzzing with a greater variety of insect life than ever before.

171

Trapped in amber

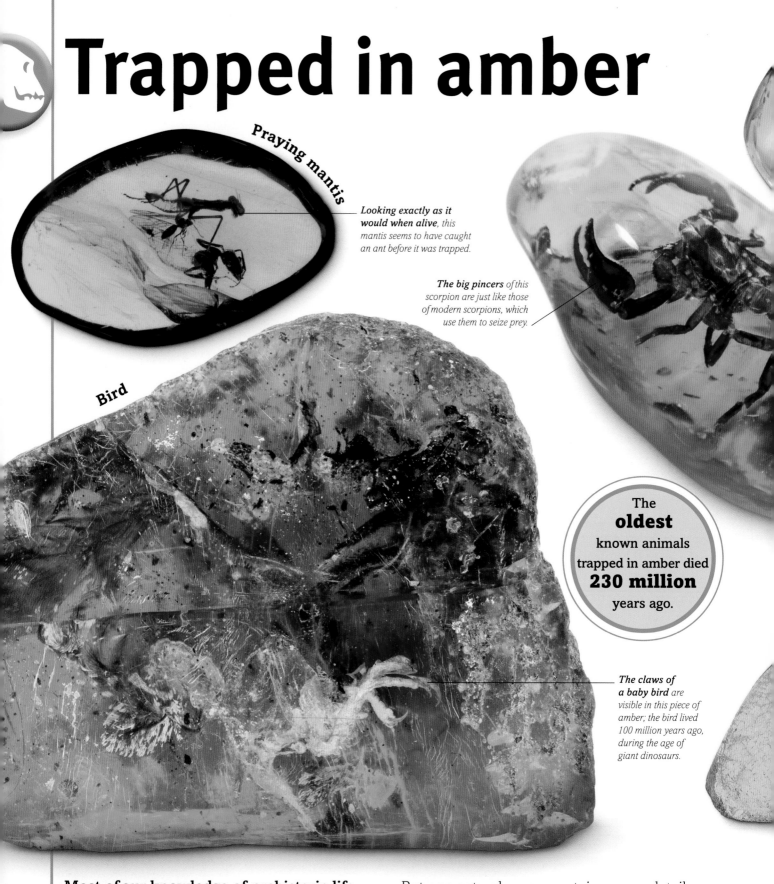

Praying mantis
Looking exactly as it would when alive, this mantis seems to have caught an ant before it was trapped.

The big pincers of this scorpion are just like those of modern scorpions, which use them to seize prey.

Bird

The **oldest** known animals trapped in amber died **230 million** years ago.

The claws of a baby bird are visible in this piece of amber; the bird lived 100 million years ago, during the age of giant dinosaurs.

Most of our knowledge of prehistoric life comes from fossils – the remains or traces of animals, plants, and other living things that have turned to stone. Usually, only the toughest materials such as bones get fossilized this way, and all the softer tissues are lost.

But one natural process retains every detail of even the smallest animals – preservation in amber. A glass-like, golden-yellow material, amber is the hardened form of sticky resin that oozes from wounds in the bark of trees like pines. Any insect that lands on it may get stuck,

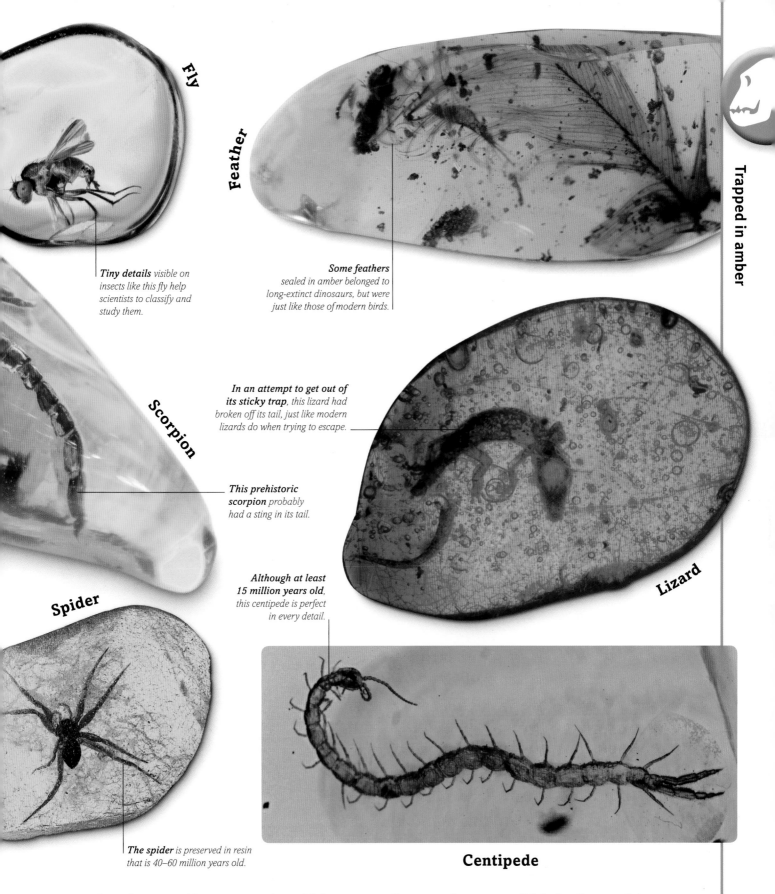

Fly

Tiny details visible on insects like this fly help scientists to classify and study them.

Feather

Some feathers sealed in amber belonged to long-extinct dinosaurs, but were just like those of modern birds.

Scorpion

This prehistoric scorpion probably had a sting in its tail.

In an attempt to get out of its sticky trap, this lizard had broken off its tail, just like modern lizards do when trying to escape.

Lizard

Although at least 15 million years old, this centipede is perfect in every detail.

Spider

The spider is preserved in resin that is 40–60 million years old.

Centipede

trapped, and covered by more resin, which kills it. This resin slowly becomes solid, and over millions of years turns into glassy amber, with the insect sealed inside it. Many kinds of small creature have been found preserved in amber, including insects, **spiders**, **centipedes**, frogs, and even small **birds**. Some of these animals were trapped so long ago that they would have lived alongside the giant dinosaurs. But most amber is more recent, dating from about 44 million years ago, early in the age of mammals.

The first mammals

Fruitafossor

Fruitafossor *was a squirrel-sized burrowing animal.*

This insect-eater may have used its strong front limbs to break into termite nests.

Sinodelphys

This earliest known pouched mammal lived 125 million years ago in what is now China.

Zalambdalestes

The long back legs of this insect-eating mammal were adapted for hopping like a rabbit.

Eozostrodon

The short limbs of Eozostrodon *suited life in burrows, where it hid away from predatory dinosaurs during the day.*

The earliest mammals appeared in the Late Triassic Period, about 205 million years ago. Over the next 140 million years mammals lived in the shadow of their dinosaur neighbours. They were small, probably nocturnal creatures that spent most of their time hiding in dense undergrowth, or even underground, preying on insects and small animals. The largest of these secretive creatures, **Repenomamus**, was no bigger than a badger. The earliest mammals – animals like **Morganucodon** and **Eozostrodon** – would have laid eggs like their

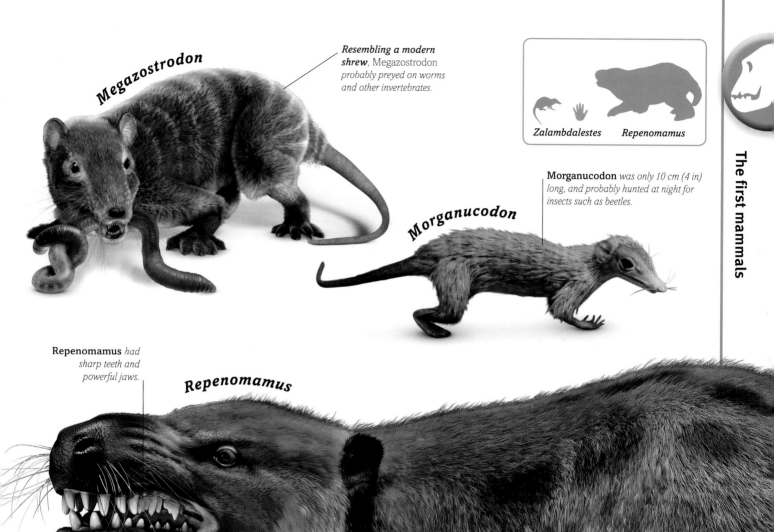

Megazostrodon

Resembling a modern shrew, Megazostrodon probably preyed on worms and other invertebrates.

Zalambdalestes   *Repenomamus*

Morganucodon *was only 10 cm (4 in) long, and probably hunted at night for insects such as beetles.*

Morganucodon

Repenomamus *had sharp teeth and powerful jaws.*

Repenomamus

One **fossil** of *Repenomamus* shows the remains of a baby dinosaur in its stomach.

The short, strong legs *enabled Repenomamus to forage for food across a wide area.*

reptile ancestors and like the modern platypus. Living mammals that breed like this are called monotremes. But later in the Mesozoic Era, animals like **Sinodelphys** started bearing live young in the same way as modern kangaroos and other pouched mammals (marsupials).

Placental mammals, which bear well-developed babies, appeared a little later, about 90 million years ago. All three types of mammal survived the mass extinction that ended the Mesozoic Era, and the survivors became the ancestors of all modern mammals.

Giant sloths and armadillos

Megalonyx

The fossils of this heavily built ground sloth have been found in North and Central America.

Megalonyx had a blunt snout.

The **shells** of *Glyptodon* were big enough for early humans to use as **shelters**.

Unlike a modern armadillo, Glyptodon had a rigid, dome-shaped shell with no flexible sections.

With rings of bony armour, the tail could be used as a weapon – possibly against rival Glyptodons.

The long claws were about 4 cm (1½ in) thick and would have been used to collect plant food.

Glyptodon

Stout claws may have been used to dig up insects, but plants formed most of its food.

Fearsome spikes of bone could have caused serious injury to an attacker or rival.

Doedicurus

While the giant dinosaurs were still alive, mammals were a small part of the wildlife. But the mammals that survived into the new era inherited a world with very few big animals, and over time their descendants started taking over the role themselves. Some of the most primitive mammals to achieve great size were the xenarthrans – the anteaters, sloths, and the armadillos and their relatives. Like their modern counterparts, they lived in South America, although some spread to North America when the two continents eventually became

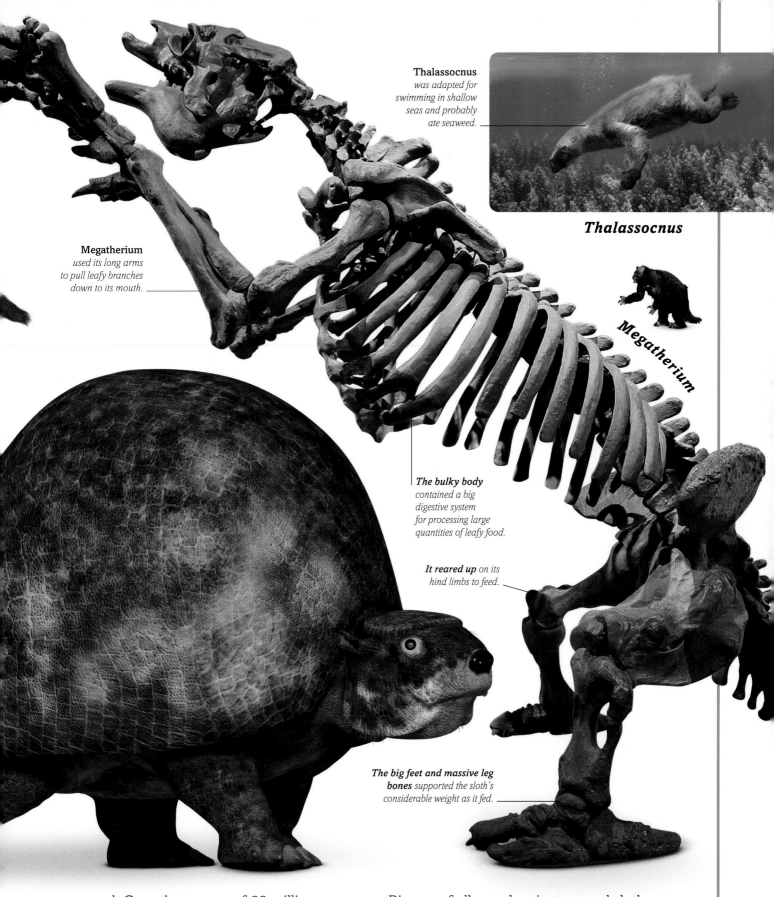

Thalassocnus
was adapted for swimming in shallow seas and probably ate seaweed.

Thalassocnus

Megatherium
used its long arms to pull leafy branches down to its mouth.

Megatherium

The bulky body *contained a big digestive system for processing large quantities of leafy food.*

It reared up *on its hind limbs to feed.*

The big feet and massive leg bones *supported the sloth's considerable weight as it fed.*

connected. Over the course of 66 million years until the end of the last ice age, they gave rise to some spectacular animals. These included the enormous, armadillo-like plant-eater **Glyptodon** and the heavily armed **Doedicurus**, which were both protected from predators by bony armour.

Biggest of all was the giant ground sloth **Megatherium**, a specialized leaf-eater that grew to the size of an Indian elephant. Able to rear up on its hind legs to reach high into the trees, it gathered food with its long front claws and mobile lips.

Body cover

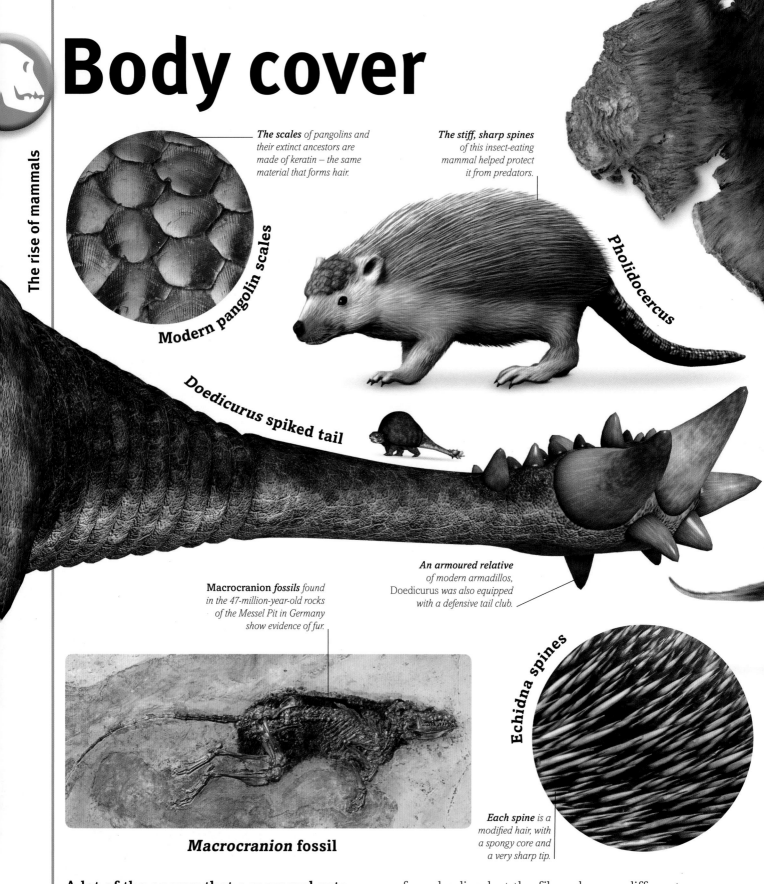

The scales of pangolins and their extinct ancestors are made of keratin – the same material that forms hair.

Modern pangolin scales

The stiff, sharp spines of this insect-eating mammal helped protect it from predators.

Pholidocercus

Doedicurus spiked tail

Macrocranion *fossils found in the 47-million-year-old rocks of the Messel Pit in Germany show evidence of fur.*

An armoured relative *of modern armadillos, Doedicurus was also equipped with a defensive tail club.*

Macrocranion fossil

Echidna spines

Each spine *is a modified hair, with a spongy core and a very sharp tip.*

A lot of the energy that a mammal gets from its food is turned into heat that keeps its body warm. The less heat it loses through its skin, the less it has to eat, so most mammals are covered with hair or fur that acts as insulation. Other animals like bumblebees have furry bodies, but the fibres have a different structure. Only mammals have true hair, and it evolved early in their ancestry, probably more than 250 million years ago. Some of the earliest physical evidence is seen in 125-million-year-old fossils of **Eomaia**, which show traces of fur

Mylodon hide

Palaeochiropteryx

The fur *of this ground sloth is so well preserved that it was once thought the animal might not be extinct.*

Armour fossil fragments

Bats *such as the 47-million-year-old Palaeochiropteryx flew on wings of naked, stretched skin.*

The tough armour *of Glyptodon was made up of hundreds of bony plates called osteoderms.*

Glyptodon

The fossils of Eomaia *are some of the earliest to be found with traces of fur.*

Eomaia

Glyptodon was about the **size** and **shape** of a Volkswagen **Beetle**.

Glyptodon *had powerful claws for climbing and digging.*

around the bones. Actual fur has been found on fragments of **Mylodon** hide preserved for more than 12,000 years in cold, dry South American caves. Hair can be modified to form prickly spines for defence, as in echidnas and the hedgehog-like **Pholidocercus**, which lived

47 million years ago. Other fossils preserve the armour of armadillo-like animals such as **Glyptodon** and **Doedicurus**, and the fossils of some extinct mammals show traces of tough, overlapping scales like those of a modern pangolin.

Mega-marsupials

Thylacoleo

Palorchestes

This horse-sized herbivore used its small trunk-like nose to gather leaves from bushes and low trees.

Thylacosmilus

The size of a lioness, and with an extremely powerful bite, Thylacoleo was the biggest ice-age Australian predator.

The huge sabre teeth of this South American hunter were protected by bony plates extending from the lower jaw.

This relative of the modern Tasmanian devil was a ferocious predator and scavenger, with very powerful jaws.

Sarcophilus

Thylacinus

Many early mammals were marsupials – mammals whose half-formed young live in the mother's pouch until fully developed. Marsupials were thriving in South America and Australia, which had once been part of the same continent, about 100 million years ago. Some, like the fearsome sabre-toothed **Thylacosmilus** and the hyena-like **Borhyaena**, continued to live in South America alongside placental mammals (mammals that give birth to well-developed young). But there were no placental mammals in Australia, so marsupials

LARGEST MARSUPIAL

The giant wombat *Diprotodon* was the largest marsupial that ever lived. Up to 3.8 m (13 ft) long, it stood almost 1.7 m (6 ft) tall. It had enormous front teeth that it used to rip the leaves off bushes and trees, and big cheek teeth for mashing the leaves to a pulp.

Diprotodon

Procoptodon

About 3 m (10 ft) tall, the biggest species of Procoptodon *was the largest-known kangaroo; it lived until about 50,000 years ago.*

This enormous marsupial *was a relative of the modern wombat and koala, and like them it ate plants.*

Stripes may have acted as camouflage *in wooded habitats, concealing the animal from its prey.*

The skull and jaws *of* Thylacinus *were very similar to those of a wolf.*

Like modern kangaroos, *the mother carried her baby in a pouch until it could feed itself.*

The heavily built Borhyaena *lived about 16 million years ago in Argentina.*

The **last** known *Thylacinus* **died** in a zoo in Hobart, Tasmania, in **1936**.

Borhyaena

evolved to take their place. They included ancestral koalas, the plant-eating, tapir-like **Palorchestes**, and the predatory marsupial lion **Thylacoleo**. During the ice ages, some of these animals grew to huge sizes, like the giant kangaroo **Procoptodon** and the hippopotamus-sized wombat **Diprotodon**. Most of these ice-age marsupials had become extinct by about 30,000 years ago, probably because climate change had created a drier climate, but **Thylacinus**, also known as the Tasmanian wolf, survived into the early 20th century.

Giant herbivores

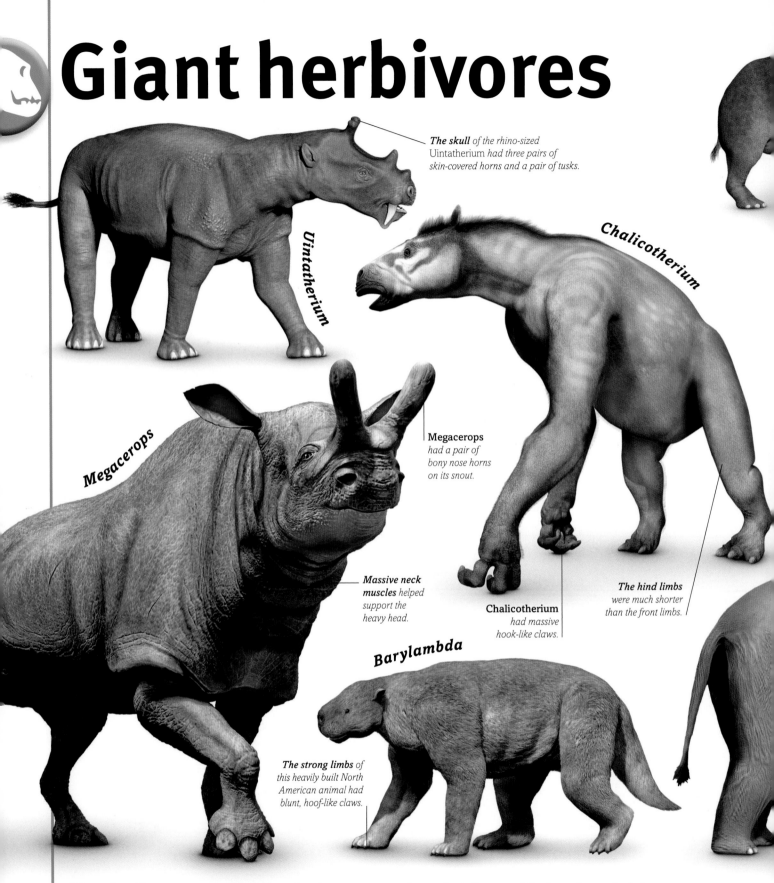

The skull of the rhino-sized Uintatherium *had three pairs of skin-covered horns and a pair of tusks.*

Uintatherium

Chalicotherium

Megacerops

Megacerops *had a pair of bony nose horns on its snout.*

Massive neck muscles *helped support the heavy head.*

Chalicotherium *had massive hook-like claws.*

The hind limbs *were much shorter than the front limbs.*

Barylambda

The strong limbs *of this heavily built North American animal had blunt, hoof-like claws.*

After the disappearance of the giant dinosaurs about 66 million years ago, most mammals were still quite small. But over time, new types evolved and replaced the huge plant-eaters that had vanished from the Earth. Fossils dating from after 60 million years ago show that the world's forests and plains were becoming populated by a range of spectacular herbivores. These eventually included the early elephant **Gomphotherium** and the odd-looking **Chalicotherium**, with its long claws that forced it to walk on its knuckles. Some of the biggest of

Moeritherium

The enlarged lip and nose formed a short trunk.

Gomphotherium

The extra pair of tusks in the long, lower jaw were used for ripping bark and stripping leaves.

Paraceratherium was the **biggest** land mammal that has **ever lived**.

Palaeomastodon

This elephant ancestor lived 35 million years ago and had four short tusks.

Paraceratherium

The massive, pillar-like legs supported the weight of this colossal mammal.

these animals are known as megaherbivores – **Paraceratherium** was 5.5 m (18 ft) tall and could reach high into the treetops like a giraffe. Despite their immense size, the megaherbivores were preyed upon by heavily armed hunters like the sabre-toothed cats. Most of these plant-eating giants have now vanished – they flourished right up until the end of the most recent ice age about 11,500 years ago – but a few megaherbivores, like the elephants, rhinos, hippopotamuses, and giraffes, still survive in some parts of the world.

Horns and antlers

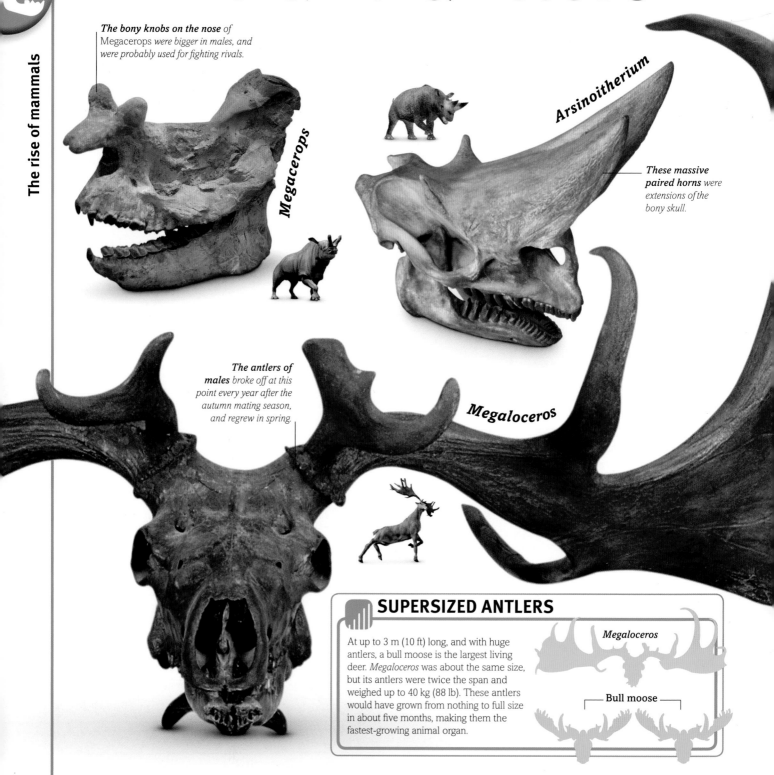

The bony knobs on the nose of Megacerops *were bigger in males, and were probably used for fighting rivals.*

Megacerops

Arsinoitherium

These massive paired horns were extensions of the bony skull.

The antlers of males broke off at this point every year after the autumn mating season, and regrew in spring.

Megaloceros

SUPERSIZED ANTLERS

At up to 3 m (10 ft) long, and with huge antlers, a bull moose is the largest living deer. *Megaloceros* was about the same size, but its antlers were twice the span and weighed up to 40 kg (88 lb). These antlers would have grown from nothing to full size in about five months, making them the fastest-growing animal organ.

Megaloceros

— Bull moose —

Many of the big plant-eating mammals that replaced the giant dinosaurs had spectacular horns and other structures on their heads. Some, like the long, sharp horns of *Pelorovis*, may have helped the animals defend themselves against hungry predators. But others were definitely for fighting with their own kind, or simply showing off. Among many modern mammals, possessing the biggest set of horns is a mark of high status, ensuring breeding success. There is no reason why extinct mammals would be any different. Since

Synthetoceras

This antelope-like animal had a Y-shaped horn on its nose as well as two horns above its eyes.

The colossal nose horn of Elasmotherium was made of keratin, like human fingernails.

Elasmotherium

The antlers were made of bone, and were covered with velvety skin when they were growing.

The name **Megaloceros** means **"great horn"**.

The bony horns – each up to 1 m (3 ft) long – would have been extended by sheaths of tough keratin.

One of the largest wild cattle that ever existed, Pelorovis lived in Africa until about 12,000 years ago.

The skull of a male Uintatherium bore three pairs of big bony knobs.

Uintatherium

Pelorovis

the animals with the most impressive headgear were more likely to breed, the horns got bigger over time, resulting in huge structures like the paired bony horns of **Arsinoitherium**, and the massive single horn of **Elasmotherium**. But the biggest horns of all belonged to the giant deer **Megaloceros**. They were antlers – horns that are shed and regrown each year. These antlers could span 3.6 m (12 ft). Only males had them, and they were used to impress and, if necessary, fight rival males trespassing on their breeding territory.

Powerful predators

Barbourofelis

Andrewsarchus

The jaw had flesh-piercing teeth at the front, but bone-crushing teeth at the back.

Big plates of bone extending from the lower jaw protected the very long, fragile canine teeth.

Each foot had four toes tipped with small, blunt hooves.

Arctodus

At about 3.4 m (11¼ ft) long, Arctodus was the largest bear ever known.

Ursus spelaeus

Also known as the cave bear, Ursus spelaeus *lived at the same time as ice-age humans, and was probably one of their most dangerous predators.*

The giant herbivores that took the place of extinct plant-eating dinosaurs were preyed upon by a variety of big, heavily armed hunters. The earliest of these were dog-like animals called creodonts like **Hyaenodon**, which was probably the fastest predator of its time. But by about 11 million years ago, these animals had been displaced by the true carnivores – the group that now includes cats, dogs, bears, and hyenas. The most fearsome of these hunters – **Barbourofelis** and the sabre-toothed cat **Smilodon** – had long,

Epicyon

A powerful, heavily built predator, Epicyon was about 1.5 m (5 ft) long.

The giant dog *Epicyon* **weighed** as much as a modern **grizzly bear**.

Armed with bone crushing jaws *that were studded with sharp teeth,* Hyaenodon *could easily pierce flesh.*

Hyaenodon

Smilodon

Smilodon *would have used its long, saw-edged sabre-teeth like daggers to stab and kill its prey.*

The front legs *were unusually powerful, and would have been used for grappling big animals to the ground.*

knife-like canine teeth for stabbing their big prey. Other carnivores such as the massively built short-faced bear **Arctodus** and the bone-crushing dog **Epicyon** probably relied on brute strength to overcome their prey. But creodonts and carnivores were not the only hunters.

One of the biggest land predators that ever existed was the wolf-like **Andrewsarchus**, which lived about 40 million years ago – a hoofed animal whose closest living relatives are wild pigs.

187

Mammal teeth

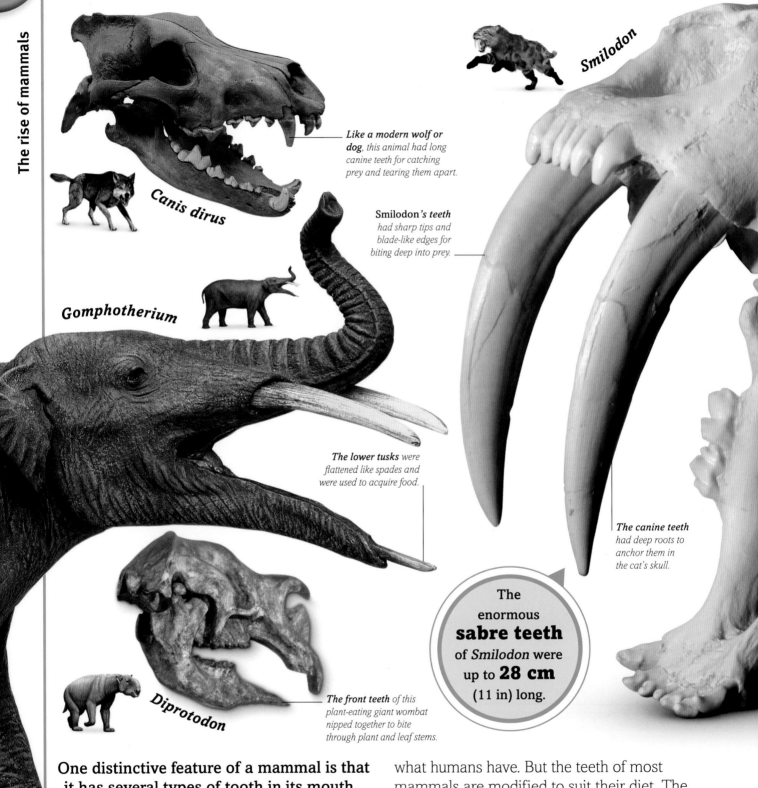

Smilodon

Canis dirus

Like a modern wolf or dog, this animal had long canine teeth for catching prey and tearing them apart.

Smilodon's teeth had sharp tips and blade-like edges for biting deep into prey.

Gomphotherium

The lower tusks were flattened like spades and were used to acquire food.

The canine teeth had deep roots to anchor them in the cat's skull.

Diprotodon

The front teeth of this plant-eating giant wombat nipped together to bite through plant and leaf stems.

The enormous **sabre teeth** of *Smilodon* were up to **28 cm** (11 in) long.

One distinctive feature of a mammal is that it has several types of tooth in its mouth. The basic arrangement is several nipping incisor teeth at the front, four pointed canine teeth adapted for gripping and tearing, and flattened cheek teeth for chewing. This is what humans have. But the teeth of most mammals are modified to suit their diet. The dire wolf, **Canis dirus**, had longer canines for seizing prey, and some of its cheek teeth were shearing blades for slicing meat. Sabre-toothed cats like **Smilodon** had huge canine teeth,

The tusks were probably used for display and gathering food, like the tusks of modern elephants.

Woolly Mammoth

Cheek tooth

Huge, flattened cheek teeth mashed the mammoth's fibrous plant food into a pulp.

Coelodonta

The cheek teeth acted like scissor blades to slice through flesh.

The cheek teeth of a woolly rhinoceros were like the teeth of horses, with high crowns for chewing plants.

WIDE GAPE

Sabre-toothed cats had to open their mouths incredibly wide to attack large prey. A modern lion's lower jaw can rotate by 70°, but *Smilodon* could manage 120°. This helped it use its sabre-teeth like daggers to bite into its victim's throats.

120° — *Smilodon*

70° — Lion

meat-slicing cheek teeth, and no chewing teeth at all. The plant-eating woolly rhinoceros **Coelodonta** had no canines but had large cheek teeth for grinding tough vegetation. A mammoth had giant chewing teeth, and its incisors had become tusks. Marsupials like **Diprotodon** had a pair of very long lower incisors that grew forwards from the lower jaw to meet the upper front teeth. All these adaptations, and more, have been inherited by modern mammals, ranging from wolves and lions to elephants and kangaroos.

SABRE CHARGE
Two hundred years ago, soldiers on horseback charged at enemies while brandishing curved swords called sabres. Twenty thousand years earlier, the big cat *Smilodon* attacked its prey with a pair of huge canine teeth that had the same blade-like form – long, slender, and sharp-edged. *Smilodon* used its sabre teeth to bring down formidable prey.

Sabre-toothed cats like *Smilodon* lived in an era of giant plant-eating mammals known as megaherbivores. These included many extinct animals as well as ancestral elephants, rhinos, and bison. Although tempting targets for big predators, these animals were hard to kill because of their size and strength. But *Smilodon* was built for the job, with immensely powerful shoulders and forelimbs, as well as those terrifying teeth. It probably ambushed its prey, leaping onto them and wrestling victims to the ground with its claws. *Smilodon* would then use its long sabres to bite deep into the animal's neck, slicing through major blood vessels with surgical precision. For the victim, it would all be over very quickly.

Ice-age giants

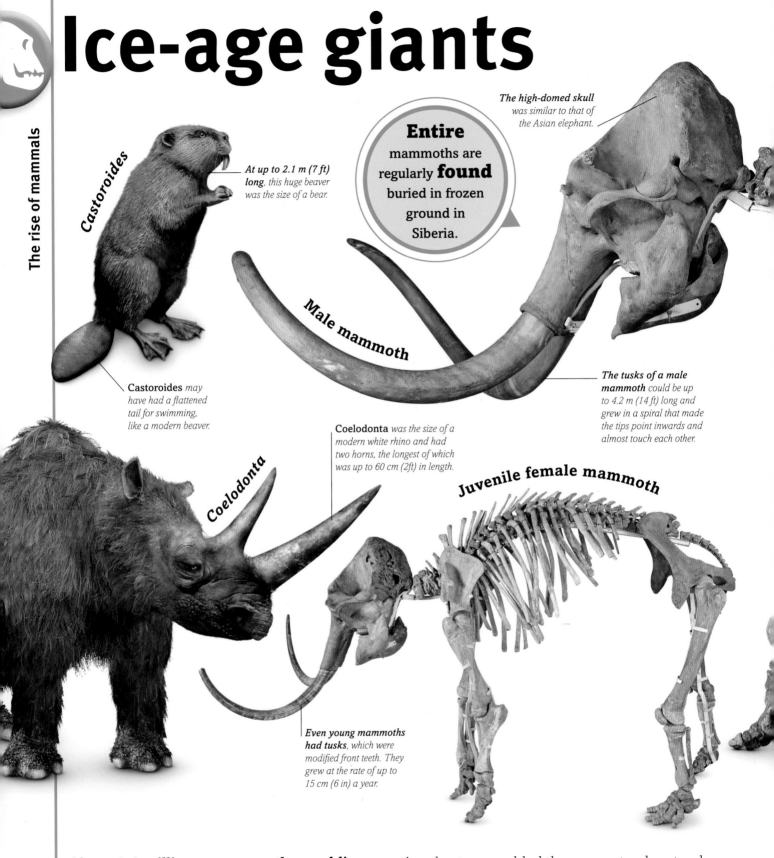

Castoroides

At up to 2.1 m (7 ft) long, this huge beaver was the size of a bear.

Castoroides *may have had a flattened tail for swimming, like a modern beaver.*

Entire mammoths are regularly **found** buried in frozen ground in Siberia.

The high-domed skull was similar to that of the Asian elephant.

Male mammoth

The tusks of a male mammoth could be up to 4.2 m (14 ft) long and grew in a spiral that made the tips point inwards and almost touch each other.

Coelodonta *was the size of a modern white rhino and had two horns, the longest of which was up to 60 cm (2ft) in length.*

Coelodonta

Juvenile female mammoth

Even young mammoths had tusks, which were modified front teeth. They grew at the rate of up to 15 cm (6 in) a year.

About 2.6 million years ago, the world's climate became cooler triggering a succession of ice ages. During these cold phases, vast ice sheets extended south from the Arctic across much of North America and northern Eurasia. The landscape beyond the ice sheets resembled the snowy, treeless tundra found today in regions like Alaska and Siberia. The southern continents were less affected because they were further from the pole. During the ice ages, many plant-eating mammals evolved a large body size as an adaptation

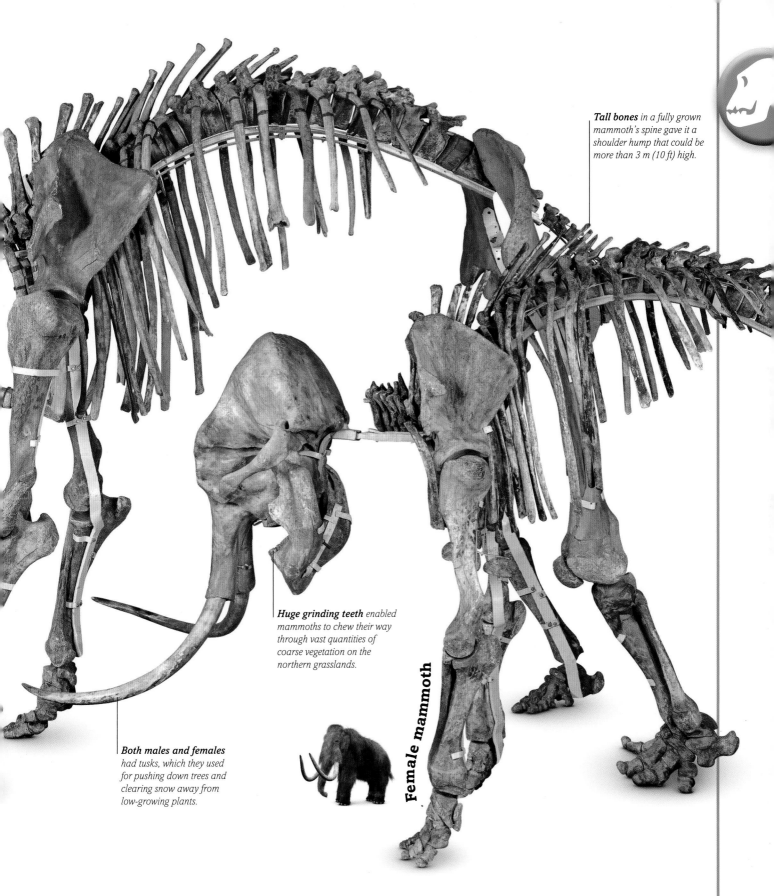

Tall bones *in a fully grown mammoth's spine gave it a shoulder hump that could be more than 3 m (10 ft) high.*

Huge grinding teeth *enabled mammoths to chew their way through vast quantities of coarse vegetation on the northern grasslands.*

Female mammoth

Both males and females *had tusks, which they used for pushing down trees and clearing snow away from low-growing plants.*

to life in the cold. The **woolly mammoth** and the woolly rhinoceros ***Coelodonta***, for instance, both had thick hair to keep out the cold, and their bulk ensured that they lost body heat less easily than smaller mammals. They lived in the northern tundra and grasslands, but other ice-age mammals, including some types of mammoth, lived further south where the climate was less harsh, or moved north only during warm periods between the coldest spells. We have been living in one of these warm periods for the last 12,000 years.

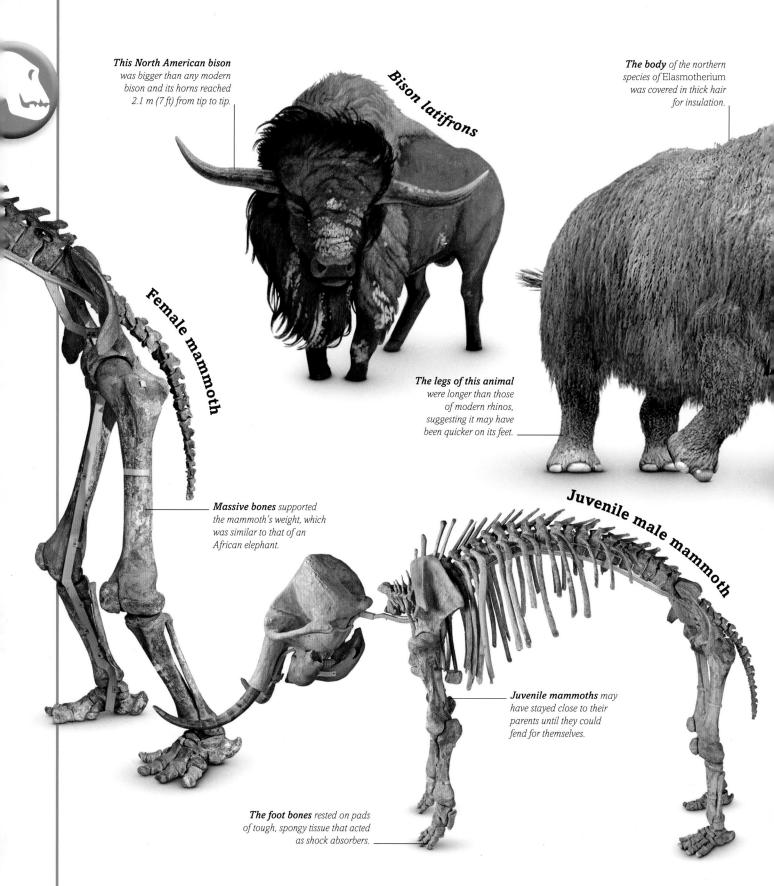

This North American bison was bigger than any modern bison and its horns reached 2.1 m (7 ft) from tip to tip.

Bison latifrons

The body of the northern species of Elasmotherium was covered in thick hair for insulation.

Female mammoth

The legs of this animal were longer than those of modern rhinos, suggesting it may have been quicker on its feet.

Massive bones supported the mammoth's weight, which was similar to that of an African elephant.

Juvenile male mammoth

Juvenile mammoths may have stayed close to their parents until they could fend for themselves.

The foot bones rested on pads of tough, spongy tissue that acted as shock absorbers.

One of the biggest ice-age giants was **Deinotherium**, a huge elephant relative with down-curved tusks in its lower jaw. It appeared about 10 million years ago but became extinct during the ice ages. Another super-sized animal was **Elasmotherium**, a type of rhinoceros that lived alongside the **woolly mammoth** in the colder parts of northern Europe and Asia. Further south there were open grasslands that provided a habitat for **bison** and other wild cattle, like the aurochs, *Bos primigenius*, an ancestor of domestic cattle. The open

No horn has been preserved as a fossil, but ice-age cave paintings indicate that it was very tall.

Elasmotherium

The name _Deinotherium_ means **"terrible beast"** in ancient Greek.

Deinotherium

Elasmotherium _had huge, flat-topped teeth, ideal for eating a diet of tough, fibrous grass that needed a lot of chewing._

The tusks grew from the lower jaw, unlike those of a modern elephant. Deinotherium _may have used them for digging or to pull down tree branches._

The enormous antlers were about 3.5 m (11 ft) from tip to tip.

Megaloceros _stood about 2.1 m (7 ft) tall at the shoulders._

Megaloceros

TAR PITS

Many fossils of ice-age mammoths have been found in a group of tar pits near Los Angeles, USA. The animals became trapped in the sticky tar and attracted predators, including sabre-toothed cats and ice-age wolves, which also became trapped. Shown above is part of a _Smilodon_ skull, blackened by tar.

woodlands of Eurasia were also home to the giant deer **Megaloceros**. The males had the biggest antlers of all time, which they used to impress females and to spar with rivals. All these animals lived at the same time as early stone-age humans, who would have hunted them for food. Many animals became extinct at the end of the last ice age, about 12,000 years ago. This was partly because of human hunters but also because changing climates eliminated many of their habitats.

Primates

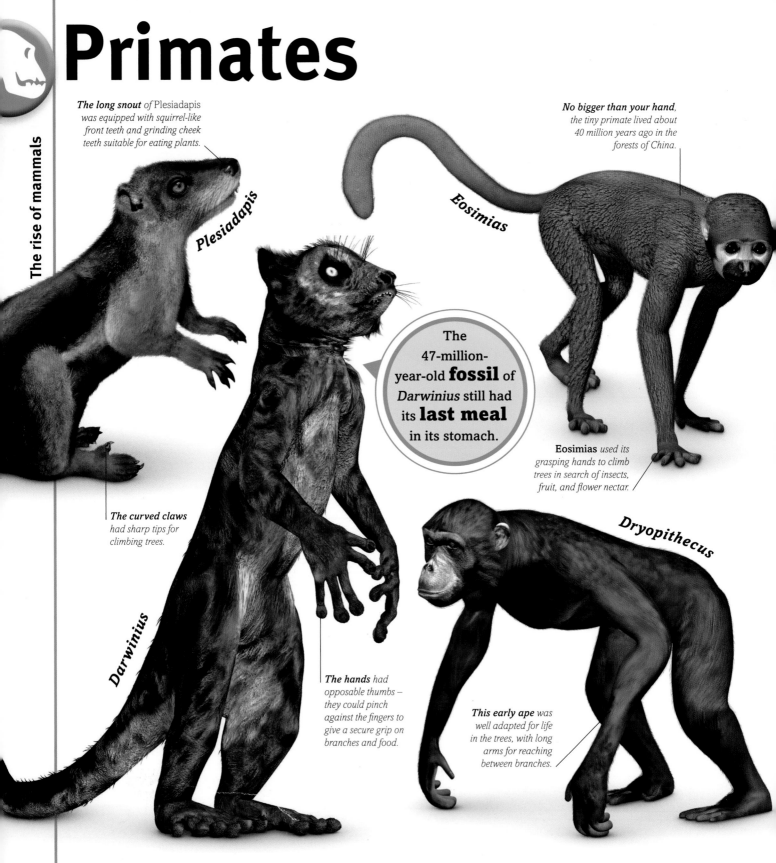

The long snout of Plesiadapis was equipped with squirrel-like front teeth and grinding cheek teeth suitable for eating plants.

Plesiadapis

Eosimias

No bigger than your hand, the tiny primate lived about 40 million years ago in the forests of China.

The 47-million-year-old **fossil** of *Darwinius* still had its **last meal** in its stomach.

Eosimias *used its grasping hands to climb trees in search of insects, fruit, and flower nectar.*

Dryopithecus

The curved claws had sharp tips for climbing trees.

Darwinius

The hands had opposable thumbs – they could pinch against the fingers to give a secure grip on branches and food.

This early ape was well adapted for life in the trees, with long arms for reaching between branches.

The first primates, such as *Plesiadapis*, appeared about 56 million years ago. They soon split into lemur-type primates, like ***Darwinius***, and early monkeys like ***Eosimias***. The oldest-known apes were alive about 25 million years ago. Their descendants were mostly tree-dwelling animals such as ***Dryopithecus***, which would have walked on all fours when on the ground. However, some later apes adapted to life on the ground by walking upright on their hind legs. They included our own ancestors.

Early humans

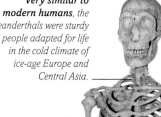

Very similar to modern humans, the neanderthals were sturdy people adapted for life in the cold climate of ice-age Europe and Central Asia.

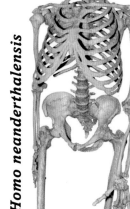

Homo neanderthalensis

Sahelanthropus

Only the skull of this North African ancestor has been found, so we cannot be sure whether it walked upright or not.

Homo habilis

Living from 4–2 million years ago, australopithecines walked upright and had a mixed diet of fruit, roots, and meat.

Australopithecus

Homo habilis *was the earliest member of our own genus,* Homo. *Its name means "handy man" – it used its hands to make stone tools.*

🔍 BIGGER BRAINS

The key difference between humans and other apes is intelligence. Our ancestors were walking upright for a while before their brains started getting bigger. As their brains grew, their jaws became smaller. The average brain size of the very early *Homo ergaster* was 850 cubic cm (52 cubic in), increasing in *Homo heidelbergensis* to 1,225 cubic cm (75 cubic in), and finally 1,350 cubic cm (82 cubic in) in modern *Homo sapiens*.

1.8 MYA–600,000 YA	600,000 YA–250,000 YA	300,000 YA–PRESENT
Homo ergaster	*Homo heidelbergensis*	*Homo sapiens*

The earliest ancestors of humans were very like *Dryopithecus*. **Sahelanthropus** may have been one of the first apes to walk upright. It lived in Africa about 7 million years ago and had a brain no larger than that of other apes. By about 3.6 million years ago, **Australopithecus** was clearly walking upright: its fossil footprints, similar to our own, have been found in East Africa. Over time, there were several *Australopithecus* species, followed by several *Homo* species. The first modern humans, *Homo sapiens*, evolved in Africa about 300,000 years ago.

WINDOW ON THE PAST
In September 1940, four teenaged boys climbed into an unexplored cave at Lascaux, southern France, and discovered scenes of prehistoric wonder – a record of animal life at least 17,000 years old. Decorated with more than 900 images, the cave walls depict herds of galloping wild horses, deer, and prehistoric cattle known as aurochs.

During the last ice age, vast areas of northern Europe were snowy tundra, but in southern France the landscape was a patchwork of forests and grasslands that supported a wealth of wild animals. They were hunted by people who were just like us, but with the different skills needed to survive at the time. The cave walls show that their abilities extended well beyond survival. The paintings were drawn by people who had studied the living animals and carried the memory of them deep into the cave. They were people with curiosity, imagination, culture, and creativity. In other words, they were among the first to show evidence of the defining feature of modern humanity – civilization.

Glossary

Adaptation
A feature of a living thing that helps it thrive in its environment and lifestyle. Adaptations are passed on to offspring and evolve over generations.

Allosauroids
A group of theropod dinosaurs that lived during the Jurassic and Cretaceous Periods.

Ammonite
A mollusc, related to squid, that had a coiled, chambered shell and lived in Mesozoic seas.

Amphibian
A cold-blooded animal that spends part of its life in water, such as a frog. They breathe through their gills in early life, but as adults they live on land and breathe air through their lungs.

Ancestor
An animal or plant species from which a more recent species has evolved.

Ankylosaurs
Four-legged, armoured, plant-eating dinosaurs with bony plates that covered the neck, shoulders, and back.

Antenna
Movable sense organ on the head of animals such as insects.

Archaea
Microscopic organisms that resemble bacteria but are only very distantly related. Some Archaea live in extreme environments, such as scalding or very salty water.

Archosaurs
A group of related reptiles that includes extinct dinosaurs, birds, pterosaurs, and crocodylians. They first appeared in the Triassic Period.

Arthropod
An invertebrate animal with a segmented body and a hard outer covering (exoskeleton). Extinct arthropods include trilobites. Living examples include insects and spiders.

Bacteria
Microscopic, single-celled organisms with no cell nuclei. Bacteria are the most abundant organisms on Earth.

Bipedal
Walking on two feet rather than four. Humans and birds are bipedal, as were many dinosaurs.

This **bony fish**, *Cladoselache*, had a skeleton made of cartilage.

Bony fish
Fish with a skeleton made of bone. Bony fish are one of the biggest groups of bony animals, or vertebrates. As well as familiar fish like tuna, herring, and salmon, the group also includes the ancestors of tetrapods.

Breeding colony
A large group of animals that has gathered to breed in one place.

Brood
In birds, to sit on eggs or nestlings to keep them warm.

Camouflage
A disguise that helps an animal to blend in with its surroundings.

Carnivore
An animal that eats meat.

Ceratopsians
Plant-eating dinosaurs, with a deep beak and a bony frill at the back of the skull. Many, including *Triceratops*, had facial horns.

Chitin
An organic substance that forms the exoskeleton of insects and other arthropods.

Compound eye
An eye formed from a mosaic of many smaller eyes. Insects have compound eyes.

Creodonts
An extinct group of flesh-eating mammals.

Cyanobacteria
Bacteria that can use sunlight to manufacture their own food by photosynthesis.

Cynodonts
A group of synapsids that arose in the late Permian (see also Synapsids).

Long shoulder spikes may have protected this **ankylosaur**, *Sauropelta*, from predators.

Dromaeosaurs
A group of bird-like, two-legged, carnivorous dinosaurs. Dromaeosaur fossils have been found on every continent.

Embryo
A plant, animal, or other organism in an early stage of development from an egg or a seed.

Era
A very long span of time. Eras are divided into shorter spans called Periods. The Mesozoic Era, for example, is divided into the Triassic, Jurassic, and Cretaceous Periods.

Evolution
The gradual change of species over many generations as they adapt to their changing environment.

Exoskeleton
An external skeleton. Animals such as crabs have an exoskeleton. In contrast, humans have an internal skeleton.

Extinction
The dying-out of a plant or animal species. Extinction can happen naturally as a result of competition between species, changes in the environment, or natural disaster.

Filaments
Thin, hair-like structures.

Fossil
The remains of something that was once alive, preserved in rock. Teeth and bones are more likely to form fossils than softer body parts, such as skin.

Fossilization
The process by which dead organisms turn into fossils. Fossilization often involves replacement of the original organism with rock minerals.

Frond
A leaf that is divided into many parts. For example, the leaf of a fern or a palm.

Sinornithosaurus was a bird-like **dromaeosaur** with feathers on its arms and legs.

Gravity
The force of attraction that pulls objects to the ground.

Hadrosaurs
Also known as duck-billed dinosaurs. Large, bipedal and quadrupedal plant-eaters from the Cretaceous Period. They had a duck-like beak that was used for browsing on vegetation.

Herbivore
An animal that eats plants.

Ice age
A period of time during which global temperatures fall and sheets of ice (glaciers) cover large areas of land.

Ichthyosaurs
A group of marine reptiles that first appeared in the Triassic Period. Ichthyosaurs had streamlined bodies similar to present day dolphins. They became extinct before the end of the Cretaceous Period.

Iguanodontians
Large, plant-eating dinosaurs that were common in the Early Cretaceous Period.

Invertebrates
Animals without backbones.

Jawless fish
A class of primitive vertebrates that flourished mainly in early Paleozoic times. They include extinct groups and the living hagfish and lampreys.

Keratin
A tough structural protein in hair, feathers, scales, claws, and horns.

Leaflet
A small, leaf-like part of a divided leaf.

Lobed-finned fish
A type of fish that has fleshy, muscular fins. Lobe-finned fish were the ancestors of all four-limbed vertebrates, including humans.

Mammal
An animal that is warm-blooded, covered in hair, and suckles its young.

Mammoth
A type of elephant with long tusks that lived during the Pliocene and Pleistocene. During the last ice age, some mammoths developed long hair, which helped them stay warm.

Marsupials
A group of mammals in which offspring are born in an undeveloped state and typically continue to grow inside a pouch on the mother.

Mesozoic
The era of time that includes the age of dinosaurs. It began 252 million years ago and ended 66 million years ago.

Microbe
Short word for "microorganism".

Microorganism
Any living creature that is too small to see without a microscope.

Monotremes
Egg-laying mammals, including the platypus and the echidnas (spiny anteaters). This egg-laying habit is thought to be the original mode of reproduction for mammals.

Lambeosaurus was a plant-eating **hadrosaur** that lived in western North America about 76 million years ago.

Mosasaurs
Giant, sea-dwelling lizards that lived during the Cretaceous Period. They were fierce predators with slender bodies, long snouts, and flipper-like limbs.

Omnivore
An animal that eats both plant and animal food. Examples include pigs, rats, and human beings.

Ornithomimosaurs
Bird-like dinosaurs that were built like ostriches. They were the fastest animals on land in the Cretaceous Period.

Oviraptorosaur
A theropod dinosaur with a beak and feathered arms, named after *Oviraptor*.

Pachycephalosaurs
A group of related bipedal dinosaurs with thickened dome-like skulls.

Paleontologist
A scientist who studies the fossil remains of plants and animals.

Palps
A pair of segmented, arm-like structures in the mouthparts of some invertebrates, such as spiders and scorpions. Also called pedipalps.

Eosimias, a tiny prehistoric **primate**, was only about 5 cm (2 in) long.

Predator
An animal that hunts and kills other animals for food.

Prey
An animal that is killed and eaten by another animal.

Primates
A group of related mammals that includes lemurs, monkeys, apes, and human beings.

Primitive
At an early stage of evolution.

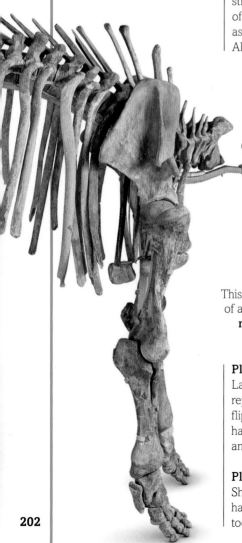

This is the skeleton of a juvenile male **mammoth**.

Plesiosaurs
Large, prehistoric marine reptiles that swam with flipper-shaped limbs. Many had enormously long necks and tiny heads.

Pliosaurs
Short-necked plesiosaurs that had large heads and powerful, toothed jaws.

Prosauropods
A group of related plant-eating dinosaurs that lived in the Triassic and Jurassic. Prosauropods were the ancestors of sauropods.

Protofeathers
Hair-like structures that provided insulation and later evolved into feathers.

Pterosaurs
Flying reptiles that lived during the age of dinosaurs. The wings of pterosaurs consisted of sheets of skin stretched between the limbs. Some pterosaurs were huge.

Quadrupedal
Walking on four legs. Most mammals and reptiles are quadrupedal.

Rachis
The central, hollow shaft of a feather.

Ray-finned fish
A major group of bony fish that includes about 25,000 of today's fish species and many prehistoric species. Ray-finned fish have fins consisting of skin stretched over a fan of thin bones.

Reptile
Modern reptiles are cold-blooded animals with scaly skin and that typically reproduce by laying eggs. Lizards, snakes, turtles, and crocodiles are reptiles. Dinosaurs and their relatives are reptiles too, but were very different from living kinds.

Sauropods
Gigantic, long-necked, plant-eating dinosaurs. The sauropods lived through most of the Mesozoic Era.

Scutes
Bony plates with a horny covering set in the skin of certain reptiles to protect them from predators.

Sedimentary rock
The type of rock in which fossils are found.

Species
A group of similar organisms that can breed with one another to produce offspring.

Spinosaurid
A large theropod dinosaur that had crocodile-like jaws for eating fish, named after *Spinosaurus*.

Spore
A microscopic structure produced, often in large numbers, by plants (except seed plants), fungi, and many microorganisms, from which a new individual can grow. Spores are usually spread by wind or water.

Stegosaurs
Plant-eating, quadrupedal dinosaurs with two tall rows of bony plates running down the neck, back, and tail.

Synapsids
A major vertebrate group, also known as "mammal-like reptiles", that branched off early in the evolution of tetrapods, and eventually gave rise to the mammals.

Tentacle
A long, bendy arm-like body part that aquatic animals use for touching and grasping.

Tetrapods
Vertebrates with four limbs (arms, legs, or wings). All amphibians, reptiles, mammals, and birds are tetrapods.

Therizinosaurs
A group of unusual-looking dinosaurs that lived in the

Cretaceous Period and perhaps the Jurassic too. Therizinosaurs were tall with small heads, stumpy feet, and pot bellies.

Theropods
A large branch of the dinosaur family tree made up mostly of predators. Theropods typically had sharp teeth and claws. They ranged from hen-sized creatures to the colossal *Tyrannosaurus*.

Titanosaurs
Very large, four-legged plant-eating dinosaurs. The titanosaurs were sauropods and included perhaps the largest land animals ever.

Trackway
A trail of fossilized dinosaur footprints.

Tundra
Treeless regions dominated by low-growing, cold-tolerant plants.

Tyrannosaurids
A group of related tyrannosaurs that are

Dubreuillosaurus was a horse-sized **theropod** that lived in the Jurassic Period.

especially large and have short arms with two-fingered hands. *Tyrannosaurus* is the most famous member of the group.

Tyrannosaurs
A group of related theropod dinosaurs that includes tyrannosaurids and all of their close relatives.

Vertebrae
The bones that make up the backbone of an animal such as a dinosaur.

Vertebrates
Animals with an internal bony or cartilaginous

skeleton including a skull and a backbone. Fish, amphibians, reptiles, birds, and mammals are all vertebrates.

Warm-blooded
Warm-blooded animals maintain a constant internal body temperature, regardless of the external temperature.

Wingspan
The distance from the tip of one wing to the tip of the other when both wings are outstretched.

Fossils of this reptile-like **vertebrate**, which lived 338 million years ago, were found in West Lothian, Scotland.

Index

Coelophysis

Euoplocephalus

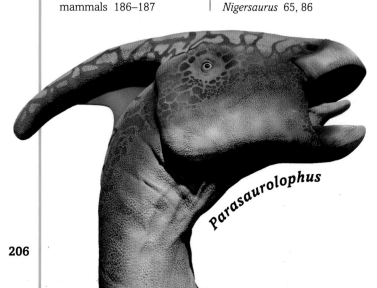

Parasaurolophus

Smilodon

ACKNOWLEDGEMENTS

The publisher would like to thank the following people for their help with making the book: Priyanjali Narain for editorial assistance; Rabia Ahmad, Meenal Goel, and Mahua Mandal for design assistance; Charlotte Webb for proofreading; and Carron Brown for indexing.

With special thanks to illustrator James Kuether

The publisher would like to thank the following for their kind permission to reproduce their photographs:

(Key: a-above; b-below/bottom; c-centre; f-far; l-left; r-right; t-top)

2-3 Getty Images: Ira Block / National Geographic. **4 123RF.com:** Nicolas Fernandez (l). **5 James Kuether:** (br). **6 123RF.com:** Corey A Ford (tr). **Dorling Kindersley:** American Museum of Natural History (tl). **7 Alamy Stock Photo:** Stocktrek Images, Inc. (tr, br). **Nobumichi Tamura:** (bc). **8 Nobumichi Tamura:** (c). **Dorling Kindersley:** Lynton Gardiner / The American Museum of Natural History (cr). **James Kuether:** (cl, cb). Science Photo Library: Sinclair Stammers (bl). **9 123RF.com:** Corey A Ford (clb). **Dorling Kindersley:** Jon Hughes (c); Oxford Museum of Natural History (bl); Harry Taylor / Hunterian Museum University of Glasgow (tr). **James Kuether:** (cla). **10 James Kuether:** (cb). **11 iStockphoto.com:** dottedhippo (cb). **13 Alamy Stock Photo:** PjrStudio (clb). **Dorling Kindersley:** Courtesy of Dorset Dinosaur Museum (tl). **Dreamstime.com:** Marcio Silva / Mbastos (tr). **Science Photo Library:** Natural History Museum, London (cr); Sinclair Stammers (c). **14 Dorling Kindersley:** Lynton Gardiner / The American Museum of Natural History (tl). **James Kuether:** (br). **15 Getty Images:** De Agostini Picture Library (cr). **James Kuether:** (cb, tr, clb, tl). **16 Science Photo Library:** TAKE 27 LTD. **17 Dorling Kindersley:** Harry Taylor / Hunterian Museum University of (br). **Dreamstime.com:** Derekteo (tr). **Science Photo Library:** Henning Dalhoff (cr, cb, ca). **18-19 Alamy Stock Photo:** BIOSPHOTO. **20 123RF.com:** Ilona Sapozhnikova (bl). **20-21 Getty Images:** James L. Amos (c). **22 Alamy Stock Photo:** Juniors Bildarchiv GmbH (bl). **22-23 Dorling Kindersley:** Senckenberg Gesellshaft Für Naturforschung Museum (t). **23 Nobumichi Tamura:** (br). **24 James Kuether:** (c, br). **25 James Kuether:** (cla, crb). **28-29 Masato Hattori**. **30 Alamy Stock Photo:** The Natural History Museum (cb). **Science Photo Library:** Dr. Gilbert S. Grant (tr). **30-31 Science Photo Library:** Chase Studio (b). **31 123RF.com:** Nicolas Fernandez (tl). **Getty Images:** De Agostini Picture Library (bc). **Science Photo Library:** Frans Lanting, Mint Images (tr). **32 James Kuether:** (tl). **33 Alamy Stock Photo:** National Geographic Creative (tl). **James Kuether:** (bl). **Nobumichi Tamura:** (ca). **34-35 Alamy Stock Photo:** All Canada Photos. **36 Alamy Stock Photo:** National Geographic Creative (br). **37 Dorling Kindersley:** Oxford Museum of Natural History (r). **38 Masato Hattori:** (ca). **James Kuether:** (t). **Nobumichi Tamura:** (br). **39 James Kuether:** (cra). **Science Photo Library:** Millard H Sharp (cb). **40 Alamy Stock Photo:** Sabena Jane Blackbird (tr). **James Kuether:** (tl). **Nobumichi Tamura:** (br). **40-41 James Kuether:** (c). **41 123RF.com:** Linda Bucklin (tr); Corey A Ford (b). **Getty Images:** Stocktrek Images (cra). **iStockphoto.com:** Warpaintcobra (crb). **43 Masato Hattori:** (tl). **44 123RF.com:** Corey A Ford (l). **Dorling Kindersley:** Oxford Museum of Natural History (tc); Oxford Museum of Natural History (bl). **45 123RF.com:** Corey A Ford (cr). **Dorling Kindersley:** Colin Keates / Natural History Museum, London (bl, tc). **46 123RF.com:** Corey A Ford (c). **Alamy Stock Photo:** Corbin17 (tr); The Natural History Museum, London (bc). **47 Alamy Stock Photo:** Sabena Jane Blackbird (tr); The Natural History Museum, London (tl). **Getty Images:** Markus Matzel / ullstein bild (br). **Science Photo Library:** Gilles Mermet (bl). **48-49 Studio 252MYA:** Lucas Lima. **50 James Kuether:** (b). **Science Photo Library:** Pascal Goetgheluck (clb). **51 iStockphoto.com:** scigelova (cr). **James Kuether:** (tr). **Nobumichi Tamura:** (cra). **52-53 James Kuether:** (ca). **52 Dorling Kindersley:** John Holmes - modelmaker / Natural History Museum, London (b); Harry Taylor / Natural History Museum, London (tr). **53 Dorling Kindersley:** Institute of Geology and Palaeontology, Tubingen, Germany (cr). **54 James Kuether:** (tr). **55 James Kuether:** (br). **56-57 Getty Images:** Arthur Dorety / Stocktrek Images. **58-59 James Kuether**. **60 James Kuether:** (cl). **Nobumichi Tamura:** (b). **60-61 James Kuether:** (c). **61 Nobumichi Tamura:** (tl, br). **62 James Kuether:** (cr, bl). **63 Nobumichi Tamura:** (bc). **64 123RF.com:** Mark Turner (cr). **Alamy Stock Photo:** ZUMA Press, Inc. (tl). **James Kuether:** (bl). **65 123RF.com:** Mark Turner (tr, cl). **Nobumichi Tamura:** (tl). **66 123RF.com:** Mark Turner (bl). **James Kuether:** (bc). **67 James Kuether:** (cl). **Nobumichi Tamura:** (tl). **69 James Kuether:** (l). **70 James Kuether:** (br). **71 James Kuether:** (bc, tr). **72-73 Alamy Stock Photo:** robertharding (c). **Getty Images:** milehightraveler (bc). **72 James Kuether:** (bl). **Reuters:** David Mercado (bc). **Science Photo Library:** University Corporation for Atmospheric Research (clb). **73 Alamy Stock Photo:** Carver Mostardi (bc); Jill Stephenson (crb). **James Kuether. 74 123RF.com:** leonello calvetti (tl). **Egidio Viola:** (cl). **75 123RF.com:** Corey A Ford (tr). **Dorling Kindersley:** Colin Keates / Natural History Museum, London (br). **Science Photo Library:** Jose Antonio Penas (tl). **76 James Kuether:** (bl, clb, br). **77 Dorling Kindersley:** Lynton Gardiner / The American Museum of Natural History (br). **James Kuether:** (crb). **Dr Lida XING:** (tl). **78-79 Science Photo Library:** Jose Antonio Penas. **80 123RF.com:** leonello calvetti (bl). **Alamy Stock Photo:** Stocktrek Images, Inc. (br). **James Kuether:** (tl). **81 123RF.com:** Corey A Ford (tr). **82 James Kuether:** (c). **83 Dorling Kindersley:** American Museum of Natural History (tr). **James Kuether:** (cr). **84 James Kuether:** (tl, tr). **84-85 James Kuether:** (c). **85 Dreamstime.com:** Tonny Wu (br). **86 Dorling Kindersley:** Colin Keates / Natural History Museum, London (ca); Oxford Museum of Natural History (bc). **Getty Images:** Bill O'Leary / The Washington Post (tr). **James Kuether:** (tc, clb, c, bl). **87 Dorling Kindersley:** Robert L. Braun (br); Colin Keates / Natural History Museum, London (cl, c); Courtesy of Dorset Dinosaur Museum (cla). **88 James Kuether:** (tr, tl, bl). **89 123RF.com:** Corey A Ford (br). **Dorling Kindersley:** Royal Tyrrell Museum of Palaeontology, Alberta, Canada (bl). **Masato Hattori:** (bl). **90 123RF.com:** chastity (bl); Corey A Ford (tl); Michael Rosskothen (br). **Alamy Stock Photo:** CGElv Austria / Elvele Images Ltd (bc). **91 123RF.com:** Corey A Ford (cra). **Getty Images:** Ira Block / National Geographic (tl). **James Kuether:** (bl, br, cla). **92 123RF.com:** leonello calvetti (tr). **Dorling Kindersley:** Courtesy of Dorset Dinosaur Museum (tc); John Downs / John Holmes - modelmaker / Natural (cra). **93 Dorling Kindersley:** Colin Keates / Natural History Museum, London (cra); State Museum of Nature, Stuttgart (br). **Masato Hattori. Nobumichi Tamura:** (cb, bl). **94-95 Alamy Stock Photo:** John Cancalosi. **96 123RF.com:** Corey A Ford (bc). **Alamy Stock Photo:** Oleksiy Maksymenko Photography (br). **James Kuether:** (bl). **Nobumichi Tamura:** (tc). **96 Dorling Kindersley:** Royal Tyrrell Museum of Palaeontology, Alberta, Canada (cl) **97 James Kuether:** (tr). **Nobumichi Tamura:** (tl). **97 Dorling Kindersley:** Peter Minister and Andrew Kerr (b) **98 James Kuether:** (cl, br). **99 James Kuether:** (tr, bc, tl). **100-101 Alamy Stock Photo:** MasPix. **102 James Kuether:** (b). **103 Alamy Stock Photo:** Mohamad Haghani (cr). **Getty Images:** Stocktrek Images (br). **James Kuether:** (tl). **104 James Kuether:** (t, br). **105 Alamy Stock Photo:** CGElv Austria / Elvele Images Ltd (br). **Masato Hattori:** (tr). **James Kuether:** (tl). **106 James Kuether:** (tr, cr, cl, cb, bl). **107 Dorling Kindersley:** Lynton Gardiner / The American Museum of Natural History (cl). **James Kuether:** (tr, br). **108 Alamy Stock Photo:** AA World Travel Library (cr). **James Kuether:** (cb, tr, cra). **Dorling Kindersley:** Natural History Museum, London (ca, br) **109 Getty Images:** Crazytang (tr). **James Kuether:** (cr, cb). **Dorling Kindersley:** Colin Keates / Natural History Museum, London (crb), Oxford Museum of Natural History (tl), Royal Tyrrell Museum of Palaeontology, Alberta, Canada (cla) **110 James Kuether:** (tl, br, cr, bc). **111 Dreamstime.com:** Shutterfree (c). **James Kuether:** (tr, bl, tl). **112-113 Getty Images:** (background). **114 © cisiopurple/cisiopurple.deviantart.com:** (tl). **115 Alamy Stock Photo:** Xavier Fores - Joana Roncero (tr). **James Kuether:** (c). **Nobumichi Tamura:** (br). **115 Dorling Kindersley:** Royal Tyrrell Museum of Palaeontology, Alberta, Canada (tl) **116 © cisiopurple/cisiopurple.deviantart.com:** (tl, tc, tr). **Masato Hattori:** (bl). **116-117 © cisiopurple/cisiopurple.deviantart.com:** (c). **117 © cisiopurple/cisiopurple.deviantart.com:** (cr). **Masato Hattori:** (tr). **Nobumichi Tamura:** (br). **118 James Kuether:** (bl, br). **119 Alamy Stock Photo:** The Natural History Museum (cb). **James Kuether:** (tr, bl). **120-121 Alamy Stock Photo:** Larry Geddis (background). **122 Nobumichi Tamura:** (bl). **122-123 © cisiopurple/cisiopurple.deviantart.com:** (c). **123 © cisiopurple/cisiopurple.deviantart.com:** (br). **James Kuether:** (tr). **124 Getty Images:** Walter Geiersperger / Corbis (cr). **James Kuether:** (bc, br). **125 James Kuether:** (tl). **Science Photo Library:** Dirk Wiersma (ca/claw). **126 Alamy Stock Photo:** Stocktrek Images, Inc. (bl). **James Kuether:** (tl). **126-127 James Kuether:** (c). **127 Nobumichi Tamura:** (tl). **128-129 James Kuether. 130-131 Alamy Stock Photo:** Stocktrek Images, Inc.. **132 Dorling Kindersley:** Courtesy of Dorset Dinosaur Museum (br). **James Kuether:** (bl, crb). **133 Dorling Kindersley:** Colin Keates / Natural History Museum, London (tc); Senckenberg Gesellshaft Für Naturforschung Museum (cr). **The Field Museum:** © Velizar Simeonovski, The Field Museum, for the UT Austin Jackson School of Geosciences. (tr). **Getty Images:** Bernard Weil / Toronto Star (cl). **134 123RF.com:** Alessandro Zocchi (tl). **Alamy Stock Photo:** Stocktrek Images, Inc. (bl). **Getty Images:** John Weinstein / Field Museum Library (c). **135 123RF.com:** Elena Duvernay (br); Corey A Ford (cl). **Alamy Stock Photo:** Stocktrek Images, Inc. (bl). **Science Photo Library:** juliu (t). **136 Alamy Stock Photo:** Mohamad Haghani (l); Stocktrek Images, Inc. (tr). **137 Getty Images:** Spencer Platt (bl). **James Kuether:** (tr). **140 Chen Yu:** (br). **Science Photo Library:** Jaime Chirinos (tl, tr); Mikkel Juul Jensen (bl). **141 Getty Images:** Daniel Eskridge / Stocktrek Images (br). **Nobumichi Tamura:** (cl). **142 James Kuether:** (bc). **Science Photo Library:** Jaime Chirinos (l); Millard H Sharp (br). **142-143 Alamy Stock Photo:** Stocktrek Images, Inc. (c). **143 James Kuether:** (br). **Science Photo Library:** (bc); Jaime Chirinos (tc, tr). **144-145 123RF.com:** Corey A Ford. **146-147 Alamy Stock Photo:** Stocktrek Images, Inc. **148 Alamy Stock Photo:** Daniel Borzynski (br); Natural Visions (bl). **Science Photo Library:** Mark P. Witton (tl). **149 Alamy Stock Photo:** Archive PL (t). **Masato Hattori:** (br, bl). **150 Getty Images:** Sergey Krasovskiy (tl, bl). **Nobumichi Tamura:** (br). **150-151 123RF.com:** Mark Turner (c). **151 Alamy Stock Photo:** Stocktrek Images, Inc. (bc). **Getty Images:** Sergey Krasovskiy (t, cr). **154 Alamy Stock Photo:** National Geographic Creative (bl). **Getty Images:** Antonio Scorza / AFP (tr). **James Kuether:** (tl). **154-155 Alamy Stock Photo:** dpa picture alliance (bc). **155 Getty Images:** Sergey Krasovskiy (br). **James Kuether:** (tr). **Nobumichi Tamura:** (cr). **156-157 Masato Hattori**. **158 123RF.com:** kampwit (bc). **Science Photo Library:** Millard H Sharp (bl). **159 Dorling Kindersley:** Senckenberg Gesellshaft Für Naturforschung Museum (br). **160 Masato Hattori:** (bl). **James Kuether:** (tl). **Nobumichi Tamura:** (tr). **161 123RF.com:** Michael Rosskothen (cr). **Dorling Kindersley:** Jon Hughes (tr). **James Kuether:** (bl, cla). **162 123RF.com:** Corey A Ford (tl). **Dorling Kindersley:** Colin Keates / Natural History Museum, London (ca). **James Kuether:** (tr, cr, bl, br). **163 Alamy Stock Photo:** Scott Camazine (ca). **James Kuether:** (b, tl). **164 123RF.com:** Corey A Ford (bl); Eugen Thome (clb). **Dorling Kindersley:** Gary Kevin / Bristol City Museum and Art Gallery (cl). **James Kuether:** (tr, br). **165 iStockphoto.com:** dottedhippo (cr). **James Kuether:** (tr, cl). **166-167 Science Photo Library:** Jaime Chirinos. **168-169 Getty Images:** Stocktrek Images. **170 Alamy Stock Photo:** The Natural History Museum (br, bl). **Rienk de Jong:** (tl). **171 Depositphotos Inc:** Pshenichka (bl). **Science Photo Library:** BARBARA STRNADOVA (tl). **Senckenberg:** (cl, tr). **172 Getty Images:** The Image Bank (tl). **Dr Lida XING:** (bl). **173 Alamy Stock Photo:** John Cancalosi (br); PjrStudio (tl). **Getty Images:** Lonely Planet Images (cr). **Courtesy Dr Enrique Peñalver and Ricardo Pérez de la Fuente:** (tr). **174 Masato Hattori:** (b). **Science Photo Library:** Michael Long (cr). **175 Alamy Stock Photo:** Magdalena Rehova (cr). **Dorling Kindersley:** Peter Minister and Andrew Kerr / Dreamstime.com: (tl). **176 123RF.com:** William Roberts (t). **Getty Images:** Roman Garcia Mora / Stocktrek Images (cl). **176-177 James Kuether:** (bc). **177 Alamy Stock Photo:** Mauro Toccaceli (r). **James Kuether:** (cra). **Science Photo Library:** Roman Uchytel (cr). **178 123RF.com:** Thittaya Janyamethakul (tl). **Dorling Kindersley:** Harry Taylor / Natural History Museum, London (bl). **James Kuether:** (ca, c). **Nobumichi Tamura:** (tr). **179 Alamy Stock Photo:** The Natural History Museum (tl); Gianni Muratore (tc). **Depositphotos Inc:** heavyrobbie (br). **Dorling Kindersley:** Harry Taylor / Natural History Museum, London (ca). **Nobumichi Tamura:** (tr). **180 Alamy Stock Photo:** Gerry Pearce (bc). **Science Photo Library:** Jaime Chirinos (l); Julius T Csotonyi (cr). **Roman Uchytel:** (tr). **181 Science Photo Library:** Mauricio Anton (tl); Michael Long (tr). **Roman Uchytel:** (br). **182 123RF.com:** Mark Turner (bl). **James Kuether:** (tl). **Nobumichi Tamura:** (br). **183 Dorling Kindersley:** Natural History Museum, London (tr). **James Kuether:** (tl). **Nobumichi Tamura:** (bl). **184 123RF.com:** Corey A Ford (tc); Mark Turner (ca). **Alamy Stock Photo:** Roberto Nistri (tl); Stocktrek Images, Inc. (bc). **Dorling Kindersley:** Harry Taylor / Natural History Museum, London (bl, cra). **185 123RF.com:** Derrick Neill (br). **James Kuether:** (tr, bc, cra). **185 Dorling Kindersley:** Harry Taylor / Natural History Museum, London (bl) **186 Dorling Kindersley:** Natural History Museum, London (cl). **James Kuether:** (br). **Science Photo Library:** Mauricio Anton (bl); Roman Uchytel (tl). **187 James Kuether:** (b). **Science Photo Library:** Roman Uchytel (tl, cra). **188 Alamy Stock Photo:** Roberto Nistri (tl). **Dorling Kindersley:** Colin Keates / Natural History Museum, London (bc). **James Kuether:** (tr). **Science Photo Library:** Mauricio Anton (bl). **188-189 Alamy Stock Photo:** Robert Malone (cr). **189 Alamy Stock Photo:** PLG (bc). **Dorling Kindersley:** Jon Hughes (cb); Harry Taylor / Natural History Museum, London (ca). **190-191 Science Photo Library:** Roman Uchytel. **192 Dorling Kindersley:** Jon Hughes (bl). **194 Alamy Stock Photo:** Stocktrek Images, Inc. (tc). **195 123RF.com:** Steven Cukrov (br). **Alamy Stock Photo:** Stocktrek Images, Inc. (bl). **James Kuether:** (tl, r). **196 James Kuether:** (bl). **197 Alamy Stock Photo:** Cro Magnon (bl); Martin Shields (tr). **Dorling Kindersley:** Oxford Museum of Natural History (br/Homo ergaster, br/Homo heidelbergensis, br/Homo sapiens); Harry Taylor / Hunterian Museum University of Glasgow (tc). **Science Photo Library:** Philippe Plailly (tl). **198-199 Alamy Stock Photo:** Hemis. **201 James Kuether:** (br). **207 James Kuether:** (tr)

Cover images: Front: **123RF.com:** Corey A Ford bl/ (Meganeura); **Alamy Stock Photo:** Mohamad Haghani fclb/ (Yi qi), National Geographic Creative tl, Stocktrek Images, Inc. bl/ (Titanis); **Chen Yu:** cra/ (Hongshanornis); **Dorling Kindersley:** Jon Hughes crb/ (Mixosaurus), Senckenberg Gesellshaft Für Naturforschung Museum tc; **Dreamstime.com:** Anetlanda ca/ (Scorpion), Tonny Wu tr/ (Mantellisaurus); **Getty Images:** Walter Geiersperger / Corbis cb/ (Therizinosaurus hand claw); **Science Photo Library:** Pascal Goetgheluck cb/ (Eryops); Back: **Depositphotos Inc:** CoreyFord clb; **Dorling Kindersley:** John Holmes - modelmaker / Natural History Museum, London cra/ (Westlothiana), Natural History Museum, London br, Oxford Museum of Natural History cla/ (Alethopteris), fcra/ (Selenopeltis); **Nobumichi Tamura:** tl; Spine: **Dorling Kindersley:** American Museum of Natural History.

OUR WORLD IN PICTURES

BOOKS

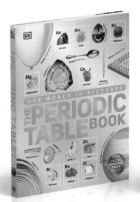
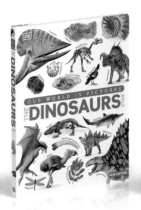
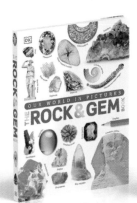

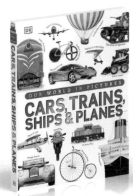
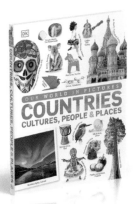
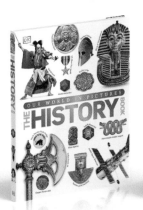

FLASH CARDS

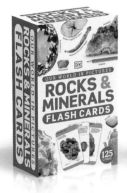
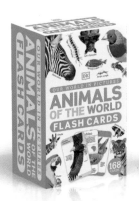
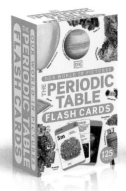
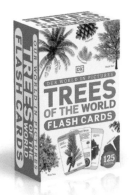

 **For the curious**